MARCUS ALLEN: SUPER RAIDER

by Chris Cobbs

illustrated with photographs

An Associated Features Book

SCHOLASTIC INC.
New York Toronto London Auckland Sydney Tokyo

Acknowledgments

The author expresses his appreciation to the
following:

Coaches Vic Player, John Robinson and John
Jackson. Writers Alan Greenberg and Jack
Disney, who reported the story with special
feeling.

The sports information office of the University of Southern California.

Dale Fetherling, Jeff Prugh and Zander Hol-
lander, for their advice and support.

PHOTO CREDITS: Cover: Focus on Sports. **vi:** UPI. **57:**
USC. **58:** UPI. **59, 60:** USC. **61:** UPI. **62:** George Gojkovich.
63, 64, 65, 66, 67: UPI.

ISBN 0-590-33375-5

12 11 10 9 8 7 6 5 4 3 2 1   10   4 5 6 7 8 9/8

Printed in the U.S.A.   01

For Lora and Matthew

CONTENTS

Marcus Allen with his Most Valuable Player Trophy at Super Bowl XVIII.

Introduction

A baby hippopotamus was born on Super Bowl Sunday 1984 at the world-famous San Diego Zoo. The 10-pound animal looked a bit like a pigskin, prompting zoo officials to name him Marcus in honor of another famous son of San Diego, Marcus Allen of the Los Angeles Raiders.

It was January 22. Three thousand miles away in Tampa, Florida, Marcus Allen and the Raiders were in their own jungle — Tampa Stadium — where they were facing the Washington Redskins in Super Bowl XVIII.

Although Allen had won the Heisman Trophy (as college football's best player) just two years earlier and had been named pro football's Rookie of the Year for 1982, his name seemed to get lost in the small print during the 1983 season. He had been overshadowed in the Los Angeles area by rookie sensation Eric Dickerson of the Los Angeles Rams and in the East by John Riggins of the Redskins.

Allen had performed superbly in the post-season games that vaulted the Raiders into the National Football League's championship game. But media attention focused on things such as the threats of Raider linemen to behead a quarterback or mash a wide receiver, and there were thousands of words written about Washington's Riggins and his massive blocking line, nicknamed "The Hogs."

The Redskins came into the Super Bowl with the league's best record and the noisy boasts of their fans ringing in their ears. But the Raiders, playing a fairly simple, straight-up, and aggressive style of defense, shut down Riggins and quarterback Joe Theismann, and got off to a 21–3 lead at halftime.

In the second half, Marcus Allen took over. After the Redskins scored, Marcus ran five yards for a touchdown and then, on the last play of the third quarter, he raced 74 yards for another touchdown, the longest run from scrimmage in Super Bowl history. The Raiders won, 38–9, and Marcus Allen was named the game's Most Valuable Player.

In the locker room, amidst all the excitement, the telephone rang. It was President Ronald Reagan, who'd watched the game on television. After congratulating Al Davis, the principal owner and driving force of the Raiders, Reagan referred to Allen as a secret weapon and a possible solution to the missile crisis in Europe. He jokingly told Allen that the Russians had called and insisted that the "secret weapon" be dismantled. Allen, who had heard his share of praise and criticism, smiled and said he thought that was nice of the President.

Later, wearing his favorite baseball cap, Allen summarized his big day, and his career, too. "A lot of people said I couldn't go the distance," he said. "I guess I proved them wrong." By any yardstick, he has proved himself the equal of any back in pro football in the 1980's.

This is the story of how Marcus Allen got there.

1

Red's Way

The comfortable stucco home, overlooking a canyon in southeast San Diego and freshened by breezes from the nearby Pacific Ocean, is more than 20 years old now. It was built by a contractor named Harold (Red) Allen at a time when both his business and his family were in the formative stages. The house has stood up well to the demands of the six children who grew up within its walls.

The care taken by Red Allen in the construction of his home is obvious. But he devoted even more attention and love to his kids. With his wife Gwen, a registered nurse, Mr. Allen treated his children to a storybook upbringing. He expected a lot, and he didn't tolerate too much mischief. But he was able to provide things many kids just dream about — like a pair of Shetland ponies, which they rode on two vacant lots next to the Allen home. There were also bicycles, piano lessons, and endless rounds of games to occupy the children.

Marcus LaMarr Allen, the second of six children (five boys and a girl) in the family, was born on March 26, 1960. His older brother Harold was named after his dad. However, Marcus acquired his name in an unusual manner — his mother picked it out of the phone book. The third child was named Damon. Next came fraternal twins, Michelle and Michael, followed by the youngster of the lot, Darius.

San Diego's mild, sunny days were perfect for a growing family with a love of games. The most gifted and energetic of the lot proved to be Marcus, who was always running up and down the steep driveway. As long as he was involved in something athletic, there was no stopping the boy. He wasn't in quite as big a hurry if there wasn't a ball involved, however. His mom always chided him for being the last one out of the house for church or school.

Marcus began playing organized football when he was about 10 years old. He could see he was better than any of his teammates, but his dad cautioned him, "Always remember there is going to be somebody else better than you." Marcus could play any position on the field, and he had an attitude of wanting to be the best. He would get mad and cry when his team lost a game.

Marcus was so in love with sports that he would return home from football practice and start playing basketball behind the house. Whenever it was his turn to do certain chores, such as washing dishes, Gwen had to go out in the yard and call for him to come inside.

There wasn't much time for the Allen kids to get into trouble, which was just the way their parents wanted it. Marcus sometimes joked that he was afraid to do anything wrong or his father would break his neck. He was exaggerating, of course, but that didn't prevent him from getting a spanking or two.

One day when Marcus was about 12, Mr. Allen was out for a walk in the neighborhood. During his walk, he happened to encounter the piano teacher who had been giving Marcus lessons.

"How's Marcus doing?" Mr. Allen asked, innocently.

The teacher looked puzzled. He hadn't seen Marcus in several months. "Why do you keep sending me the money for the lessons?"

Marcus had been skipping his lessons without letting his parents know. When his dad got home, he administered the last spanking of Marcus' childhood. Marcus was getting too big for physical punishment.

He wasn't too big for Red Allen to control, however.

The summer when he was 12 years old, Marcus was the star shortstop on his Little League baseball team. One afternoon at practice, the manager asked him to move to center field, just for the day. Marcus, who could be pretty stubborn at times, refused. When the manager insisted, Marcus decided to strike back by asking his teammates to boycott the rest of the practice.

Boycotts are best left to adults with a cause, as the boys discovered. The team's manager, who was none other than Red Allen, had a little talk with his son. The boycott was over in a matter of minutes. And the team had a new outfielder.

The next year, when Marcus was 13, he and his older brother Harold accompanied their father to work one morning. Mr. Allen, who was still in the business of building houses, gave the boys an introduction to the pleasures of wielding a hammer. They all climbed up on the roof of a house under construction. It was midsummer, and the temperature was in the 90's.

Marcus and Harold worked for an hour or two without complaining. At last they decided to take a break. They slowly made their way down the ladder and joined their father, who was already sitting in the shade and sipping a cold soda.

"Well, fellas, what do you think?" Mr. Allen said. "Do you want a job?"

Marcus answered for both of them.

"No, thanks, Dad," he said. "I think I want to go to college and get a degree when I get older. This kind of work isn't for me."

Mr. Allen laughed. That was just what he wanted to hear. He always stressed the value of education to his boys. Along with his wife, he talked to them about the examples of great leaders, such as Dr. Martin Luther King. Marcus made up his mind to be somebody great and make his parents proud.

2

A Man Among Boys

It was late afternoon, nearly sunset, and the driver of the car had to squint as he approached an intersection. Coming to a stop, the driver glanced out the window at a young man wearing a dirty football uniform. The kid had his helmet tucked under his arm and he looked tired. That look touched a sympathetic nerve in the driver, whose name was Mike Garrett. He had been a great football player at the University of Southern California. He hadn't played the game in years, but he had not forgotten the feeling of weariness after a rugged practice.

"Hey, you look beat," Garrett said. "Hop in, I'll give you a ride."

Garrett introduced himself and then asked his passenger's name.

"Marcus Allen," the grateful rider said. "I play quarterback."

Garrett asked if he was a good quarterback.

8

"Pretty good."

"Well, how good is pretty good?"

"I'm OK," Allen said. "I'm OK."

That was true, as far as it went, but it wasn't the whole truth. Marcus Allen was not only a good quarterback, he was a good defensive back, too. In fact, he played every position except center and guard during his career at Abraham Lincoln High School in southeast San Diego. He was the best player on his team, by far. But he wasn't one to brag about his skills. He didn't think that was cool.

During his years at Lincoln, a predominantly black school, Marcus was just about the coolest and most popular kid on campus. His nickname was Casper the Ghost, because of his light complexion. And he had a way of trying to make himself less visible, to blend in with his friends and teammates, when he received one of his many awards. He never was caught up in being a star athlete. "Aw, coach, why me?" he would say when called upon to receive a plaque or some honor. "Why not the rest of the guys, too?"

Vic Player, the coach at Lincoln High, treated Marcus as just one of the guys for the most part. Player approached football as a business, and his job was to win games and help his athletes do well. He told them it wasn't in their best interest for him to be a buddy. They would have to work and work hard if they expected to have a future in football at the college level.

With the good of the team in mind, Player approached Marcus before his senior season and suggested he move to quarterback. It wasn't an idea Marcus liked very much. He just wanted to be one of the guys. He seemed to rebel against the move. In practice one day he fumbled snap after snap, seemingly on purpose. He was trying to communicate his unhappiness.

The message got through, loud and clear. Coach Player saw what was happening. To let Marcus and his teammates know who was in charge, he threw Marcus off the team in a fit of disgust. "Get outta here — and don't come back!" he bellowed.

A sorry Marcus returned the next day, holding his helmet and extending his apologies. Player would have begged him to come back if he had not showed up. But the coach wasn't going to let anyone know that at the time.

"I told Marcus he would play quarterback, or not at all," Player said years later. "We needed his leadership and direction and athletic ability on the field at all times. Marcus eventually changed his mind, of course; but I don't think he liked playing quarterback, and we didn't get along very well until later in his senior year."

Why didn't Marcus want to play quarterback, the most glamorous position on the field? What lay behind his reluctance? Player can only guess, but he thinks the real reason was that Marcus was thinking years in the future. "Marcus and I both knew he was going to be a professional football player one day," Player said. "Marcus knew that there had never been a really successful black quarterback in the National Football League. So I think he was just looking at it as a businessman."

That's only a guess on the coach's part. But it's quite possible that Marcus had the ability to read the future even as a high school senior in the fall of 1977.

In any case, once he embraced the idea of playing quarterback, Marcus had a brilliant senior year. He led his team to a 12–0–1 record and the championship of San Diego County. Marcus passed for 1,434 yards and nine touchdowns. He rushed for 1,098 yards and 12 touchdowns on just 132 carries, an average of 8.3 yards every time he tucked the ball under his arm.

What's more, he continued to play defensive back. He had always been better known for his tackling ability than anything else, and he delivered 94 unassisted hits and participated in 217 others. In one game alone, he was in on 30 tackles, an astounding number for anyone, much less a player who was taking part on offense and defense. Marcus also intercepted 11 passes and returned four of them for touchdowns.

But it wasn't until the final game of the year, against Kearny High, that Marcus really came into his own. In pacing Lincoln to a lopsided 34–6 victory, he carried the ball nine times for 197 yards and had touchdown runs of 85, 30, 20, and 10 yards. He also scored a touchdown on a 60-yard interception return.

Marcus was named to *Parade* Magazine's All-

America team. He also was named the recipient of the Hertz No. 1 award as the top high school athlete in California. When he was presented this award, he got to meet his idol, former Southern Cal and professional star O.J. Simpson. Not much later, Marcus became the only player in Lincoln High School history to have his jersey retired. Number 9 will never be worn by another Lincoln athlete.

In his years at Lincoln, Marcus was a good student, compiling a 3.3 average, and was involved in numerous clubs and extracurricular activities. But nothing diverted his attention from his first love, football. Once, he was hanging out with a few friends, and one of them took some marijuana from his pocket. Marcus wasted no time finding a new group of friends.

His education at Lincoln provided more than just textbook knowledge and football training. Lincoln had experienced several years of student unrest prior to Marcus' arrival in the mid-1970's. The school had earned the nickname Maximum Security H.S. Marcus was subjected to several instances of racism during football games. He was the object of some malicious late hits and name-calling, and even a death threat, according to Coach Player. But he wasn't deterred from his pursuit of athletic excellence.

At six feet one and 185 pounds, Marcus was not the largest or the fastest member of the team. He could run the 100-yard dash in about

10 seconds flat, good for a high school athlete, but not good enough to make the sprint team at Lincoln. What set Marcus apart was all-out dedication to football, a quick mind, and an intuitive feel for the game.

"Marcus was a free spirit. He played with his whole heart, soul, and being," said Player. "Sometimes he didn't conform to everything I asked of him on the field. He didn't pay attention to everything I said, and he got beaten on a few plays because of it."

While Marcus was working out the kinks of adolescence, Player never eased up on him. Both knew Marcus was much superior to the other players on the team, and Marcus needed somebody to push him. Player had Red Allen's backing all the way in the effort to hold Marcus to high standards.

"Mr. Allen never interfered with me or acted pushy, like so many parents do," Player said. "I coached four of his sons, and he was always more insistent that they do better in academics than athletics. All of the boys had a competitive edge, and some of the same grace and speed that Marcus had."

Marcus had so much talent and drive that he sometimes overwhelmed less-talented opponents. Once, during a basketball game, the referee told him to ease up, he was too good for the other players. And during a football game, an official pleaded with him to tackle a little more gently. He wasn't a dirty tackler; but he could deliver a vicious blow, and some observers thought he was destined to be a free safety in college or pro football. That belief was underscored when he made those 30 tackles in one game.

In addition to football and basketball, Marcus was also a member of the Lincoln track team. He could high jump six feet two inches, triple jump 45 feet, and long jump 22 feet.

Despite his versatility and overall athletic talent, Marcus was not a world-class sprinter; and some people questioned whether he was fast enough to be a truly outstanding college back. It was the kind of thing he would hear several years later, when the pro scouts began looking at him, too.

Vic Player was used to having sprinters on his track team who could blaze 100 yards in 9.5 or 9.6 seconds. Because of this one seeming weakness in Marcus' arsenal of athletic skills, many people, including Player, assumed he would wind up playing defensive back, or perhaps fullback, when he got to the college level.

But Marcus possessed other gifts, such as exceptional vision and the ability to see exactly what was going on around him. These gifts would more than compensate for his lack of blistering speed. And he also had the ability to get along well with teammates and coaches. Before he left Lincoln, he became very close to Vic Player.

"I don't pretend to know how Marcus really is," Player says today. "But he has always tried to act responsibly and be a good model for young kids. He's very interested in his family and especially in his youngest brother, Darius. He once asked me to come out of retirement and coach Darius if he plays high school football." Marcus probably wouldn't mind if Lincoln let Darius wear his old jersey, Number 9.

3

Little Juice

Befitting Marcus Allen's status as the most honored high school senior in California, he had his pick of colleges. As a youngster, Marcus was thrilled by the exploits of O. J. Simpson and the University of Southern California. He had a pretty good idea of where he wanted to play one day. As he put it to friends, "There's nothing in the world like a USC football Saturday."

The USC Trojans were probably the most dominant and feared team in college football during the 1960's and 1970's. First under Coach John McKay and later under John Robinson, the Trojans appeared in 11 Rose Bowls between 1963 and 1980, and won national championships in 1962, 1967, 1972, 1974, and 1978.

The roll call of USC All-Americans reads like a Who's Who of college football. Through the years the school produced such all-time greats as Simpson, Frank Gifford, Charles White, Anthony Davis, Mike Garrett, Ricky Bell, and Lynn Swann, all of whom were All-Americans as backs or ends. And the list of blockers and defensive stars was just as impressive: Ron Yary, Charle Young, Marvin Powell, Brad Budde, and Roy Foster, to name a few.

Only a very select group of college teams — Notre Dame, Ohio State, Alabama — could rival the reputation of the University of Southern California.

Southern Cal is one of two major universities famous for their athletic programs in the city of Los Angeles, only about 120 miles from Marcus Allen's hometown of San Diego. USC, which shares the headlines in Los Angeles with UCLA and a half-dozen pro teams, plays its home games at the Los Angeles Memorial Coliseum. It was the site of both the 1932 and the 1984 Olympics, and the scene of some of the most memorable football games ever played. With a seating capacity of just under 100,000 and its distinctive peristyle end, the Coliseum was the perfect showplace for a powerhouse team like the USC Trojans. It would be hard for anyone, let alone a high school senior with an active imagination, to dream of a more spectacular setting for his college career.

Coach John Robinson had heard from people he trusted that Marcus was leaning toward USC. Still, Coach Robinson was taking nothing for granted when he paid a recruiting visit to the Allen home in San Diego. He had a list of things to tell Marcus and his family, and he went over them in his mind as he walked up the steps to the front door.

Robinson felt a few moments of nervousness, but they were quickly eased. He was at once struck by the affection the family members felt for each other. And he felt himself relaxing as he yielded to a partylike atmosphere in the Allen den.

On the wall, for anyone to see, was a plaque with the following message:

> *Be careful of the words you say,*
> *So keep them soft and sweet.*
> *You never know from day to day*
> *Which one you'll have to eat.*

Coach Robinson realized he would not have to eat any of his words. He didn't have a lot of phony recruiting promises to make. But even if he had, the family was having such a good time that he wasn't going to be able to deliver a long-winded speech.

And then the lights went out.

A power failure in the neighborhood plunged the Allen household into darkness, and the party atmosphere that existed before only got better. Gwen Allen produced candles for everyone. Then she went into the kitchen for cookies and milk. Nothing bothered the Allen family, Coach Robinson discovered. He didn't get an immediate commitment from Marcus, but he did go away that night impressed with the stability and affection of the Allen family.

Any confusion about where Marcus would wind up vanished when Marcus was introduced to his boyhood hero O. J. Simpson. They met at an awards ceremony at which Simpson was the host. Marcus asked O. J. to call his mom and say hello. "The Juice," as O. J. was known, told Gwen Allen how thoughtful her son was. After that, Oklahoma and all the rest who wanted to enroll Marcus didn't stand a chance. USC it would be.

There were a number of striking similarities between Simpson and Allen, who were both Californians. O. J. grew up in San Francisco before entering USC, winning the Heisman Trophy and going on to become the first man in professional football to gain over 2,000 yards in one season. Although he was 13 years older than Marcus Allen, The Juice was still at his playing weight of about 205 pounds when they met at that banquet in 1978. Simpson had worn Number 32 at USC. Marcus would wear Number 33, because the Trojans retired "32" when O. J. moved into the pros. Years later, Marcus would be presented with Number 32 by the Los Angeles Raiders.

Naturally, Marcus picked up the nickname "Little Juice" not long after he became a USC Trojan. And before his college days were over, he would become a part of Simpson's circle of friends, in addition to surpassing many of his records. There was a time when Marcus had to leave his silver sportscar with a mechanic for a few repairs. O. J. loaned him one of his cars. Three days later, Marcus returned it. O. J.

wasn't angry at the delay, but he suggested that in the future Marcus might want to acquaint himself with the Los Angeles public bus system.

Marcus got quite an introduction to the world of big-time collegiate football. During his freshman season, 1978, Marcus was a reserve tailback on a team that won 12 games, lost just one, and was awarded the national championship. He didn't play much, running 31 times for 171 yards (a 5.5 average) and one touchdown, but the experience of being Number 1 was still a wonderful confirmation of everything he had anticipated about Southern Cal.

Marcus had gone to USC expecting that he would be a defensive back. Based on his high school achievements and his ability to tackle fiercely, Marcus seemed like a potential star in the Trojan secondary. But just four days after the start of fall practice, in August 1978, Coach Robinson decided he would shift Marcus to tailback.

This was one move Marcus could agree to without dissent. He had hesitated about moving to the outfield as a Little Leaguer, and he had balked at becoming a quarterback at Lincoln. But tailback at USC! No way was he going to say no to his coach for making that proposal. Every kid who follows USC dreams of running to glory behind its huge blocking line.

And one day in the fall of his freshman year, Marcus told a reporter about his dream. "Anything I have accomplished has come through God. He has His own plans for me. But, you know, I would like to win that Heisman someday."

The 1978 season was certainly a nice way to get started in college football. There were victories over some of the biggest names in college football: a 24–14 win over Alabama, a 27–25 win over Notre Dame, and a 17–10 win over Ohio State in the Rose Bowl.

But a few months after the Rose Bowl, in the spring of his freshman year, Marcus came in for a rather rude shock. Coach Robinson proposed that he move from tailback to fullback. Not surprisingly, Marcus was hesitant. Being the fullback at Southern Cal means functioning almost exclusively as a blocker. The fullback might as well be a center. Nobody knows his name.

"Think about it," Coach Robinson told Marcus, "because you're not going to play much at tailback in 1979." The tailback job was reserved for a superb runner named Charles White, who had already had two exceptional years at the position. In 1977 White had rushed for 1,478 yards as a sophomore, and followed with 1,859 yards in 1978. No matter how much promise Marcus Allen showed, he wasn't going to take the job away from White.

Being a reasonable young man, Marcus thought over his coach's proposal and decided to accept it. It was explained to him that USC wanted to field the most dangerous backfield combination it could. Lynn Cain, who was the fullback in 1978, had graduated, and the coaching staff decided to give the job to Marcus. He would be following in the footsteps of some famous past Trojan fullbacks, such as Sam Cunningham and Mosi Tatupu.

"I knew Marcus was willful and had a strong personality," John Robinson said later, after he had become the coach of the Los Angeles Rams. "I had no sense that Marcus would be difficult to deal with, and he wasn't. He was all a coach could hope for. A guy with ambition will do anything, and Marcus obviously had a lot of ambition.

"At first he didn't understand how to practice. But he learned from watching Charlie White, who was just a maniac on the practice field, running out every play. And Marcus saw what it took to become a physically dominant player in college football."

Marcus had played nearly every position on the team in high school, and he had given ample proof of his willingness to play football in a very physical manner. But there was no way to prepare himself for what would happen on his first practice play as a fullback at USC. The quarterback called the play, and the Trojans moved up to the line of scrimmage. It was a running play, and Marcus' assignment was the same as it would be on almost every down in the coming season. He was the lead blocker.

Marcus had played football for years without any serious injuries, but on his first practice play as a fullback, he threw his block and felt his helmet strike his assigned target. He also felt pain in his nose. When he looked down and saw blood all over his jersey, he knew something was wrong with him. But his first reaction was to ask if anyone else was hurt. The answer was no. But Marcus himself had suffered a broken nose on his very first try as a blocker. What a way to break in! Yet Marcus proved again how tough he was by quickly returning to practice after his injury.

It was the job of backfield coach John Jackson to train Marcus as a blocker and to help him prepare for the mental adjustment. "I tried to make him realize he was a tough individual," Jackson said. "Toughness is an ingredient demanded of a USC fullback and tailback. I was his buddy, and he could come to me anytime, but I also stayed on him pretty good to make him become a good player."

Marcus might not have been thrilled with the new position, but he knew it was just temporary, and he threw himself into it with the same zeal with which he had played quarterback at Lincoln. With USC's immense line leading the way, and Marcus mopping up any linebackers or defensive backs left standing, Charlie White put together a great season in 1979. He carried the ball 332 times for 2,050 yards, a 6.2 average. And the Trojans rolled to an unbeaten 11–0–1 season that they polished off with another win in the Rose Bowl. This time they defeated Ohio State, 17–16.

Marcus became such a strong blocker that he sometimes wondered if he might have to stay at the position for the rest of his career at USC. He made the sacrifices the coaches asked, and they were pleased. In addition to blocking for White, he averaged 5.7 yards a carry in accumulating 649 yards rushing as a sophomore. He scored eight touchdowns. He also showed the versatility that had been his trademark by catching 22 passes for a 14.3 average. Included in his total was a 105-yard performance against Texas Tech when White was hurt and had to sit out the second half.

"Marcus is one of those guys you could hand a golf club for the first time, and he'd hit the ball right down the middle," Robinson said at the time. "Then he'd help you find your ball."

All in all, Marcus made quite a hit with the Trojan coaches as a sophomore. But he didn't quite live up to his own expectations. He told a reporter his goal was to gain 1,000 yards even while serving as Charles White's escort. That would have meant averaging about 10 yards every time he carried the ball. "I'm ambitious," Marcus said. "They [the coaches] want me to stick my head in there and get three yards. But I'm not a three-yard runner. I like to keep going and going."

It was just that kind of burning ambition that helped attract Coach Robinson's attention in the first place. And it was one of the qualities that would prove essential to Marcus during the trials and triumphs that lay ahead of him in his junior and senior seasons at Southern Cal.

4

Learning To Run

Spring football is a time of drudgery for the most part. There are no cartwheeling cheerleaders, no plane trips to faraway stadiums, no national television audiences. The colorful game uniforms are locked away and won't be unpacked for another six months. But the foundation for what will happen in September is laid in March and April.

If a player doesn't work diligently under the warm spring sun, he won't be in the starting lineup when the real season kicks off. The University of Southern California is less than a half hour from the shores of the Pacific Ocean, but while many students spend lazy afternoons on the beaches, the Trojan football team is hard at work.

And now, after two seasons of waiting patiently for his chance to play tailback, Marcus Allen got his wish in the spring of 1980. The great Charles White was headed for pro football. The most glamorous position in college football was awarded to a rising junior who had never stayed at any position long enough to truly master it. And even before spring practice had ended, Marcus discovered there was a great deal he would have to learn before he could expect to see his bust cast in bronze and displayed in USC's athletic center, Heritage Hall.

Coach John Robinson pushed his players, particularly his tailbacks, very hard. So much is expected of Trojan tailbacks that they must be kept fresh and injury-free, so they are spared contact drills in the fall. But not in the spring. That's when a USC tailback serves his apprenticeship and learns just how grueling the job can be. "Our practice ideas are the same as a game," Robinson told his squad. "Our tailback is going to get the football a great deal of the time. He may run 30 or 40 times in a game. And in spring practice, he is going to get the stuffing knocked out of him."

Aside from the physical pounding he absorbed that spring, Marcus also had to begin adjusting to the mental pressures of being the Southern Cal tailback. Three of the six men who preceded him at the position had won the Heisman Trophy: Mike Garrett in 1965, O.J. Simpson in 1968, and Charlie White in 1979. And the three other tailbacks hadn't done so badly themselves. Clarence Davis, Anthony Davis, and Ricky Bell all had done their parts to carry on the tradition of the USC tailback.

Coach Robinson could see Marcus had the

ambition, the magnetism, and what he called that tailback look in his eye. And he quickly began to indoctrinate Marcus on how to think about his assignment. "The tailback has to tell himself he's going to carry 40 times a game, and sooner or later, he's going to get a big play," Robinson said. "It may not happen until the 38th carry of a ballgame, but sooner or later, the big play will come. There's an ethic to the position. A work ethic. The Trojan tailback has got to have this special quality, this inner strength."

Observers of spring workouts were able to see that while Marcus didn't have the slashing style of White, the strut of Anthony Davis, or the power to intimidate in the manner of Bell, he had a fluid motion that was all his own. In his own mind, Robinson began to think of Marcus as being similar to Frank Gifford, who played at USC in the early 1950's, before starring in pro ball and then as a TV analyst alongside Howard Cosell and Don Meredith. No matter how Marcus' style was described, it was also obvious that he had to make some adjustments before he could become a true breakaway threat.

When he played fullback the previous fall, Marcus was lining up four yards behind the line of scrimmage. His assignment was to provide the lead block for the tailback five or six yards down the field. When he became the tailback, he had to learn to float up to the line of scrimmage and save his explosion for another step or two. At least that was the way O.J.

himself analyzed the change Marcus had to try to make.

It wasn't easy. It was a different style of striding. Marcus began to have trouble keeping his feet. He would approach a linebacker or a defensive back, and his feet would go out from under him. He would seem to stumble just as he was ready to try to put a fake on a potential tackler. Marcus was shown films of Simpson, who could change directions in 1/24th of a second. Marcus seemed to be just as quick. But he couldn't take full advantage of his quickness if he couldn't learn to stay balanced.

It was a definite problem, and it was one that Coach Robinson, along with backfield coach John Jackson, would need some time to solve. All through the spring, and again when fall practice began, the coaches worked with Marcus. "He could see where he wanted to go, but his body just couldn't take him there," Robinson said.

Robinson believed that Marcus had exceptional eyesight and could see things on the field that most backs couldn't. Robinson compared Allen's vision to that of Hall of Fame baseball slugger Ted Williams, who supposedly could pick up the spin of the ball an instant after it left the pitcher's hand. Marcus also had another kind of vision, which Robinson described as the ability to go into a situation and immediately see what was going on. He had a great feel for what was happening around him.

Marcus certainly got an eyeful and an earful in his first starting assignment as the Southern Cal tailback in 1980. The Trojans traveled to Knoxville, Tennessee, and defeated the University of Tennessee, 20–17, before a crowd of 95,049, the second largest ever to see a game in the South. Marcus was handed the ball 39 times and kept his feet well enough to rush for 132 yards on Neyland Stadium's artificial turf. The Trojans were able to preserve their 20-game unbeaten streak, the longest in the nation, on a long field goal with no time remaining on the clock.

The following week brought Marcus head to head with Heisman Trophy favorite George Rogers of South Carolina. In a game played at the Coliseum, the Trojan defense held Rogers in check until the fourth quarter. Rogers wound up outgaining Allen, 141 yards to 107, but USC won without a struggle, 23–13.

Although Marcus had now gained more than 100 yards in each of his first two starts, he was not in full bloom at tailback. He was continuing to experience problems with his center of gravity — problems that caused him to fall down just as he was about to break open into the secondary.

And so the lessons on the practice field intensified. Coach Robinson came up with a technical adjustment. He explained it something like this: A back needs to have his feet close together to run straight. The feet need to be a little wider when the back wants to make a cut. If the back tries to cross one leg over the other, he will have a tendency to lose his balance. So what a runner needs to do is widen his feet just for an instant as he prepares to fake out a tackler. Some runners hesitate and chop their feet, up and down. That's no good. The trick is to widen the base, then boom, accelerate past the tackler.

If that sounds a little hard to follow, well, it's even harder to put into practice. A football player can nod his head and say, "Yeah, sure, coach, I'm with you," but when he tries to execute the instructions, it's another matter altogether. And even when the concept begins to make sense, it takes hundreds of repetitions before it is so ingrained that it becomes a conditioned reflex. A running back isn't going to have time to tell himself to widen his feet every time he sees a tackler. It has to become a habit, like breathing.

Marcus applied himself diligently. Time after time, he worked on the techniques suggested by his coaches. They could see it would pay off eventually. "No matter what, Marcus was going to be successful," Robinson said. "Even if he didn't make it in football, he would have been great in some other sport. Heck, he might have won a gold medal in the luge in the Winter Olympics, or something." The point was, Allen had the right attitude, the desire to improve.

There was no magic turning point. There wasn't one game or one run when Marcus could say he had mastered the art of cutting without slipping. There were high points and low points as the 1980 season unfolded.

One of the highlights came in the third game of the year, when the Trojans flew to Minneapolis to face the Minnesota Gophers. Quarterback Gorden Adams handed the ball to him 42 times, and Marcus responded by gaining 216 yards and scoring two touchdowns in a 24–7 triumph. It was his first 200-yard game as a Trojan. It was also a performance that recalled the showing of O.J. Simpson in 1968 on the occasion of Southern Cal's last visit to Minneapolis. The Juice gained 236 yards and scored four touchdowns on a wet field that day.

Furthermore, the truth of John Robinson's words was driven home. The coach had told Allen that sooner or later, the USC tailback would wear down the enemy tacklers. And sure enough, on his 40th carry he broke off tackle for a 20-yard touchdown run. And on his 42nd run of the afternoon, he broke a tackle and went 37 yards to score. It was a satisfying afternoon.

"I knew it would be hard playing tailback, but I didn't realize how much pressure there is to the position," Allen said in the dressing room following the game. He had showed a little more flair than in his first two games at tailback, and Coach Robinson hoped the pressure would ease a bit. Already there had been suggestions from alumni and critics in the media that Marcus should be shifted back to fullback.

Looking back to the early stages of the 1980 season, it seems farfetched to realize that some doubted whether Marcus Allen had the tools to be the Trojan tailback. After all, he had exceeded 100 yards rushing in each of the first three games, and the Trojans were still unbeaten. It seems unfair, but there it was: a headline asking if USC had an average tailback.

"The world seemed to have doubts about Marcus," Coach Robinson said several years later. "But I never doubted him and, more importantly, he never doubted himself. I told him the things he needed to do to become a great tailback and one day win the Heisman. I told him it would still happen if he had faith in himself and believed he would become the best."

Even as he worked to improve his technique, Marcus also had to adjust to the expectations of his teammates. He was in the position of being a team leader, but he seemed uncertain about it. He had accepted the challenge willingly in high school, but now he seemed unsure of himself. He was a talkative, rah-rah guy at Lincoln. But when he got to USC, he left that stuff to others, including Charlie White. Now White was gone, and it was another adjustment for Marcus Allen.

On the first weekend of October, USC went up against the Arizona State Sun Devils, the last team to beat the Trojans, back in 1978. The Trojans won, 23–21, but it wasn't a very distinguished day for the team or for Marcus. He fumbled three times and averaged only a little more than 3.5 yards a carry.

One of the most interested and best informed observers of Allen's troubles was O.J. Simpson. He saw that Marcus was having some of the same problems he'd had as a developing runner. The Juice recalled that he didn't have a run of more than eight or 10 yards in his first five games at USC.

"A great offensive line, such as USC has, is going to get you five or six yards downfield," Simpson said. "A down lineman should never get you. It's how you handle that first linebacker that is so important. Marcus was stumbling a lot in that circumstance. He had to learn to get rid of the guy with a move or by shaking loose."

After a while, all the analysis began to sound pretty much the same. Marcus had reached the stage where he was going to have to let time be his ally. All the stuff he'd been told now had to be absorbed by the subconscious part of his mind. Eventually, with an athlete of his gifts, the little tricks would become second nature, and he would truly be on his way.

Midseason was now at hand for the Trojans, and the schedule sent them to Tucson for an appearance against the University of Arizona. Thus far, Southern Cal hadn't been a "big play" team, but had relied on its defense in a jam. The defense was nearly flawless as USC defeated Arizona, 27–10, to remain undefeated in its last 25 games. And Marcus had an outstanding performance, rushing 41 times for 201 yards and scoring three touchdowns. Other backs, reading about the criticism Allen was receiving, must have been pretty envious when they saw the kinds of statistics he was posting. They should have his troubles.

Trouble overtook the Trojans the next weekend in Eugene, Oregon. In an error-filled performance, the Number-2-ranked Trojans stumbled to a 7–7 tie with the lightly regarded Oregon Ducks. "We beat ourselves," Marcus Allen said after gaining 159 yards, but failing to score a touchdown. "It was a tie, but we consider it a loss."

After taking a weekend off, USC broke out of its rut by clobbering the California Golden Bears, 60–7. The win gave the Trojans a 6–0–1 record and kept alive their hopes for another national title. Along with Notre Dame and Georgia, the Trojans were now one of three remaining unbeaten teams in the country. "I'm always surprised with people who have such little faith," Coach Robinson said after the game in a comment made for the team's doubting alumni. Of course, Marcus Allen had already had a taste of it. On this occasion, when the Trojans lashed back at their critics, they didn't need Marcus as much as usual. Given the ball just 29 times, he responded with 133 yards and two touchdowns.

Marcus was now gaining confidence in the techniques that his coaches had imparted. The result was that his balance improved and he began to make great strides. "The greatness in him," Coach Robinson said, "became his ability to cut. With his exceptional eyesight, he would see a tackler and make him miss. And he had that terrific ability to compete and to understand the game so well."

It was no coincidence that USC reached its high point for the season against Stanford in game Number 8. The Trojans won, 34–7, before a sellout crowd of 84,000 at Stanford Stadium. Stanford's young quarterback, John Elway, was sacked eight times as the Trojans got back into the national title picture on a day when Notre Dame was tied. Allen gained 195 yards and scored twice. As Mal Florence of the Los Angeles *Times* wrote, "He ran with more style and authority than at any time in the season."

Marcus matched his season high of 216 yards a week later against Washington, but USC's long streak of 28 games without a loss was halted. The Huskies won, 20–10, and clinched an appearance in the Rose Bowl. The downturn in the team's fortunes continued against crosstown rival UCLA, which beat the Trojans, 20–17, and held Allen to 72 yards on 37 rushes. An eye injury that sent him to the hospital for a short time forced Marcus to miss the season's last game, a 20–3 victory over Notre Dame at the Coliseum.

At last, a trying and ultimately disappointing season was over for USC and Marcus Allen. He had made the transition to tailback and finished with a highly impressive 1,563 yards rushing, an average of 4.4 yards per carry, and 14 touchdowns. He finished second in the nation to South Carolina's Rogers, who gained 1,781 yards and won the Heisman Trophy.

Marcus also caught 30 passes for 231 yards and wound up as the Number 1 all-purpose back in the nation with an average of 179.4 yards per game.

The Trojans finished 8–2–1, a dropoff from their 12–1 and 11–0–1 records of the previous two years. Because standards were so high, it went down as a less than satisfying year. But the USC tailback had survived one of the most difficult periods of his life and established himself as a strong candidate for the Heisman Trophy in 1981, his senior year. Marcus, who was in the habit of regularly reading the Bible, often turned to Revelations — "to see how it's going to end," he told sportswriter Alan Greenberg. "I wore Number 9 in high school and they retired it. I'm gonna try to retire one here, too."

5

2,000 Yards and Beyond

In the summer between his junior and senior years at Southern Cal, Marcus Allen addressed one of the little flaws that caused some critics to pick on him every now and then. People, including his own head coach, said he was just a step slower than some of the other highly regarded backs in football. It's usually assumed that a man can do nothing about his speed. What he's born with is what he's going to have to make do with.

Marcus set out to test that theory. He ran and ran, all summer, endurance runs and sprints. In a typical workout, he would begin by jogging several miles. Then he would run six 80-yard sprints, followed by eight 60-yard dashes, six 40-yard dashes, and eight 20-yard sprints. When he reported for fall practice, he was timed in 4.6 seconds for the 40. That was about one tenth of a second faster than his previous best. It may not sound like much, but a half step or so can make the difference in gaining 10 yards or getting by the last tackler and breaking a big gainer.

John Robinson liked what he saw. He already knew Marcus wanted to be the best back in America. Here was further proof of his dedication.

"Marcus is one of the top two or three players in the country," Robinson said before the Trojans opened the season against the University of Tennessee. "He has improved as much between seasons as any player I have ever coached. Last year he didn't have the luxury of a balanced attack to help him, and he had to hammer away at people, which he did very well. But this year our offense will do more things, and he'll have more fun."

The Trojans had all the fun they could want in belting Tennessee, 43–7, to begin the new year. With a new quarterback, John Mazur, the Trojans were expected to have an improved passing game. And Mazur hit his first six throws, including a 50-yard touchdown toss, before yielding to reserves as the score grew lopsided. Allen, on the other hand, played a little longer. He was given the ball 22 times — about a third less than on a normal Saturday — and he advanced it 210 yards, an average 9.5 yards a snap. He scored four touchdowns, including one on a 55-yard run.

Tennessee coach Johnny Majors had seen another highly acclaimed back, Georgia's Herschel Walker, a week earlier in his team's season opener. Majors, who had coached a Heisman Trophy back, Tony Dorsett of Pitt, several years before, was moved to superlatives by the running of Marcus Allen.

"He covers much more ground than Herschel," Majors said. "His long and lanky physique makes him a good target for receiving and helps him in his overall running game. He picks his holes as well as any back I've seen in my coaching career."

Robinson also liked what he saw in his team's debut. "Marcus is a little quicker," he said. "He has worked hard to improve and is more mature and stronger. He's growing in confidence and is aware of what's going on. He's seeing things better. He had some nice holes, but he got to them with poise, hesitated at times, and then burst through them. He was patient."

The Trojans as a team had to be patient when they were held scoreless in the first half by Indiana in the season's second game. Marcus gained 164 yards in the first two quarters, but USC wasn't able to put the ball over the goal line. Things improved some in the second half as USC's massive line, composed of Roy Foster, Don Mosebar, Bruce Matthews, Tony Slayton, and Darryl Moore, eventually wore down the Hoosiers. The Trojans wound up with a 21–0 victory and Marcus with a career-high 274 yards and two touchdowns.

After two games Marcus was averaging 242 yards rushing, and there was talk that he might break Tony Dorsett's NCAA record of 1,948 yards set in 1976. Dorsett averaged 177 yards a game. Marcus himself seemed to think it was possible. "Some back is going to break the record," he said. "I think it is definitely achievable."

It was still early in the season, but already there were observable differences in Marcus Allen's running. "He is more animated," said USC's All-American guard, Roy Foster. "He's playing extremely hard. I wasn't sure he could run that fast, but he's doing it now. And he knows that he's the head man."

A professional scout watched Marcus and was also struck by his improvement. "He thinks like a quarterback, hits like a fullback, runs like a tailback, and catches like a wide receiver," the scout said. "He knows how defensive people react because he played there, too."

A national television audience got to see how Marcus reacted under pressure when USC faced Oklahoma at the Coliseum on the season's third weekend. It was a meeting between the nation's Number 1 and Number 2 ranked teams, and it was a classic. Oklahoma, which had held some interest for Allen when he was being recruited, led 24–14 in the fourth quarter before USC rallied for a 28–24 victory. There were 10 fumbles by Oklahoma's wishbone ground attack, but Allen and the Trojans handled the ball flawlessly. And Marcus enjoyed his third consecutive 200-yard day, gaining 208 yards on 39 carries and scoring three touchdowns.

"Marcus is the best tailback I've seen play on

this field," Coach Robinson said after the game. And he had watched Charles White, Ricky Bell, and Anthony Davis in action at the L.A. Coliseum.

Marcus was also asserting himself as a leader, something he had seemed a bit reluctant to do earlier in his college career. "Marcus said in a prayer after the game that if God stands by us, we won't blink the rest of the season," Robinson said. "And I said, 'Amen, we're Number 1.'"

Marcus never looked back the following week. He was off to the fastest start of any back in the history of college football. He gained 233 yards in a 56–22 USC triumph over Oregon State. He thus became the first college runner to gain 200 or more yards in four consecutive games. And his total of 925 yards in four games broke the four-game record of 905 set by Oklahoma's Greg Pruitt in 1971.

The numbers were staggering. In the first month of the season, Marcus had nearly twice the yardage Dorsett had gained in the first four games of his record-breaking season. And Marcus now had seven 200-yard efforts in 14 games as the Trojan tailback, breaking White's school record of six.

While the records were piling up around him, Marcus seemed to be getting more popular than ever with his teammates. But he refused to let his success alter the way he conducted his life away from football.

He liked to dress in designer jeans and a baseball cap. He seldom said anything without smiling. He didn't let too many people get intimately involved in his life, but he rarely went anywhere alone, either. He was living in an apartment in a shady neighborhood about 15 minutes from the USC campus. There was a high ceiling, a fireplace, and a regulation basketball goal next to the fireplace. Marcus liked to entertain guests by shooting hoops.

Marcus continued to work as hard as ever in practice. As Coach Robinson observed: "Our tailback must always be our most dedicated practice player. He must be as tough or tougher than anyone else on the team, and he must be willing to pay quite a price for his success in terms of effort and concentration." For his part, Marcus explained his job in simple terms. The average play takes six seconds, he said. He could run six seconds 40 times a day for 10 years if he had to.

In the season's fifth game, Marcus ran 74 yards for a touchdown, and USC built a 10–0 first-quarter lead over Arizona. It appeared it was going to be a restful afternoon. But Arizona, a 21-point underdog, allowed no more scoring and came on offensively to upset the Trojans, 13–10, and destroy USC's ranking as the Number 1 team in America. Despite a pinched nerve near his left shoulder, Marcus played most of the game and gained 211 yards, his fifth straight effort of more than 200.

Marcus Allen's fantastic streak finally was ended in the season's sixth game, but USC recovered from its upset the previous weekend to beat Stanford, 25–17. Stanford deployed its defense in an eight-man line to limit Marcus to 153 yards on 40 carries, an average of 3.8 yards per rush.

"It was bound to happen," Marcus said. "I'm not worried about getting 200 yards every week, but I want to win the game. Everyone keys on the USC tailback. Sometimes they get him and sometimes they don't. It was a tough day." It was also tough for Stanford's highly regarded quarterback, John Elway. He completed only 23 of 45 throws and was sacked six times as he experienced some of the frustration that Marcus felt in the face of so much defensive pressure.

Of all the rivalries in college football, few can match the pageantry and tradition of the USC-Notre Dame series. Through the years, the teams have produced more All-Americans, national championships, and classic match-ups than any other schools. Everybody knows the history of the Fighting Irish, from the days of the legendary coach Knute Rockne to the present. Marcus Allen knew all about the tradition of the USC-Notre Dame game, and he also knew what a physical pounding he was likely to receive. "When we meet, it's the most physical game in America," he told a New York writer the week of the game. "But we're looking forward to playing them."

Allen's confidence was infectious. His teammates could readily sense his desire. "You can see the fire in his eyes," split end Jeff Simmons said. "He was tentative last year, but now he's running like he owns the place. You get the impression that he's thinking, 'I'm good for 200 yards today, guys.'" Added guard Roy Foster: "He's running like a wild man. I've never seen him run so hard. He's running smarter, too. Seeing things and opening his eyes."

Marcus was hurt when the Trojans met Notre Dame in 1980, so he was making his first appearance against the Fighting Irish as a tail-back. Just as he predicted, Notre Dame was waiting for him. It was a hard-fought, tense game, and Marcus had to battle to gain 147 yards, well below his amazing average. While the Irish concentrated on Marcus, USC full-back Todd Spencer picked up 74 yards, includ-ing a 26-yard scoring run that provided the Trojans with a 14–7 victory. "Sometimes the defense overplays Marcus, and you have to find somebody else," Coach Robinson said in summary. Give Marcus an assist in this game.

The atmosphere was considerably different when USC overpowered Washington State, 41–17, to advance its record to 7–1 on the fol-lowing Saturday. If Marcus earned an assist against Notre Dame, he all but earned this win by himself. On the biggest day of his Trojan career, Allen piled up 289 yards on 44 carries. Despite a sore left ankle, he averaged 6.6 yards per rush and scored three touchdowns.

Washington State coach Jim Walden called him "Superman." Typical of the way he had learned to handle such talk, Marcus shrugged and said, "He must have meant the whole team." Fielding the inevitable questions about a 2,000-yard season, Marcus said, "I think our linemen want it more than I do."

Through eight games Marcus was averaging 215.6 yards a game and needed to average just 92 yards in the remaining three games to surpass the magic 2,000 mark. The 1965 Heisman Trophy winner, USC's Mike Garrett, said Marcus was running as well as O.J. Simpson, but with more power. And Coach Robinson had a hard time containing his admiration. "Charles White, Anthony Davis, and Ricky Bell were attack runners," he said. "The smoke was coming out of their ears. Marcus is developing that attacking kind of style, but like O.J., he hesitates and looks for holes. The things he's doing have never been done before."

Marcus proved the accuracy of those words in the next two games. First, against California, he rushed for 243 yards in a 21–3 win and surpassed Dorsett's NCAA single-season record of 1,948 yards. After nine games, Marcus' total stood at 1,968. It was a record-setting afternoon for Marcus, but it wasn't his best game by any means. He fumbled four times and lost two of them. His timing was off somewhat because his tender left ankle had reduced his involvement in practice since the Washington State game.

Seven days later, Marcus ventured into uncharted territory on a cold, blustery afternoon in Seattle. A 13-yard sweep on USC's first possession put him over the 2,000-yard barrier. The record-breaking run came, appropriately, on USC's most recognizable play, nicknamed "Student Body Right," when he was escorted by a gang of gargantuan blockers. But that was the climax of a miserable afternoon. The Trojans were upset, 13–3, and their chances of appearing in the Rose Bowl all but vanished. That was what bothered Marcus. He wouldn't be going to the Rose Bowl for his final appearance as a senior.

"The 2,000 yards are important because it feels good to run where no man has run before," Allen said. "But I'm hurting inside because I won't get to the Rose Bowl." After 10 games, Marcus now had 2,123 yards, an average of 212.3 per game, and was the clear-cut favorite for the Heisman Trophy.

Although Marcus had been the Number 1 high school player in California, and had produced an All-American performance in his first full season at tailback, he had entered the 1981 season with something to prove. No one really had any idea he would put together the greatest statistics of any college back in history.

One of the top judges of talent in professional football, Gil Brandt of the Dallas Cowboys, talked about Marcus Allen's remarkable achievement. "It's one of the most amazing turnabouts by a player I can ever remember," he said. "He learned to run so much better in a year's time. He is playing as well as any tailback ever has and I would not have believed it a year ago."

There was only one game left now in the regular season, and Marcus made it count. He carried 40 times and gained 219 yards in USC's spine-tingling 22–21 victory over UCLA. He established three more NCAA records and tied another, bringing his record total to 11 for the 1981 season. He now had 11 200-yard games, a career record; the best per-game rushing average for a season, 212.9 yards; and the best per-carry average, 5.81 yards. Most impressive of all was his total of 2,342 yards, the record that the future runners would be aiming for, likely for a long time to come.

The only suspense remaining now concerned the Heisman Trophy. Marcus was expected to beat out Georgia's great Herschel Walker, but he wasn't taking anything for granted. "You think I'll win it?" he often asked friends. His pals were confident, but Marcus wasn't so sure. "There seems to be a lot of Herschel-mania going around."

He seemed to be forgetting that he was the USC tailback, probably the most visible position in college football. In most matters, he had remarkable vision. But apparently, the magnitude of his position, and his accomplishments, still had not struck him with full force.

6

The Heisman Hoopla

Despite his record-breaking season, Marcus Allen was going to have to put up with a little suspense before finding out who would receive college football's most important honor. USC had ended its regular season against UCLA on November 21, and the results of the Heisman Trophy voting would not be announced until the first week of December.

Marcus knew all about Herschel Walker and Jim McMahon, his foremost challengers for the Heisman. Walker was a 225-pound All-American sophomore tailback at the University of Georgia who was fast enough as a sprinter to be considered a candidate for the U.S. Olympic track team.

McMahon was Brigham Young's All-American quarterback, who set dozens of collegiate passing records. Twelve quarterbacks had won the Heisman. Most often, however, the award had gone to running backs. But that didn't guarantee anything in 1981.

Marcus passed some of the time by flying around the country for a series of awards and interviews with newspapers and television networks. He went to New York for an appearance on *The Today Show*, but didn't even have the time to see the sights of Manhattan. Then he returned to Los Angeles to catch up on schoolwork and attend the USC football awards banquet.

A few days later he flew to a ceremony in Washington, D.C. While there, on Friday, December 4, he received a telephone call from a representative of the Downtown Athletic Club of New York, which presents the Heisman. The caller didn't tell Marcus if he'd won. He simply suggested it would be a good idea for Marcus to be in New York the next day, Saturday, December 5.

There was no turning back now. When Marcus stepped off the plane in New York, he was met by a member of the Downtown Athletic Club and taken to the group's offices in lower Manhattan. Still they were being evasive. Marcus, however, realized that his chief competition, Georgia's Herschel Walker, was not in New York that day. Herschel was playing a game in the South that afternoon.

The suspense continued to build while Allen waited in his hotel room. He remembered looking at his watch about noon. The Heisman announcement was to be made at 7 P.M. Marcus drifted off to sleep in the early hours of the afternoon. After what must have been a couple of hours, there was a knock on the door.

An official of the Downtown Athletic Club entered and told the sleepy-eyed football player the good news. "Congratulations, Marcus, you are the 47th winner of the Heisman Trophy."

In the room with him was John Jackson, the backfield coach at USC. Before the season, Marcus had told Jackson he would like to gain 2,000 yards. Jackson had told him to be realistic, to think in terms of 1,700 or 1,800 yards. Now they both realized what had happened. Together, coach and player began jumping around the room. Jackson is normally a reserved, controlled man. But not at this emotional moment.

There were still a couple of hours before the official announcement, which would be made live on national television. In the voting of the sportscasters and writers who made up the Heisman jury, Marcus Allen had been an easy winner. He received 441 first-place votes and 1,797 points (on the basis of three for first place, two for second, and one for third). Walker ended up with 152 first-place votes and 1,199 points. McMahon had 91 first-place votes and 706 points. Allen was the leader in five of the six geographical voting areas, while Walker led in the South.

After the TV show — the trophy itself would be presented a week later — Marcus conducted a press conference. He told the writers he was a goal-oriented person who had hoped to win the Heisman. He presented himself smoothly and with no trace of false modesty.

"I have found my place in history as the best player in the country at this particular time," he said. "In acting, it's the Oscar. In football, it's the Heisman. It makes me Number 1. I put in a lot of hard work, but I was not alone. My parents, my coaches, and my teammates are all responsible for this award.

"But at the risk of sounding self-centered, I would have voted for myself. It is a very happy day for me, and I am proud to become Southern California's fourth Heisman Trophy winner."

Then he paused and said he really didn't believe it yet. "Maybe I will," he said, "when I go home and pinch myself. This makes me very proud."

Wearing a stylish blue suit and surrounded by oil paintings of former Heisman winners such as Tom Harmon, Glenn Davis, Paul Hornung, and Roger Staubach, Allen said all the right things. But there was no doubting his sincerity. "I wish there were a lot of little Heismans so I could distribute them to my teammates," he said.

Jokingly, he said he felt he had almost won the Heisman twice. He was referring to his experience as Charlie White's blocking back two years before. Marcus had taken quite a beating while helping White win the Heisman.

"When he won it, I felt something special — like I was contributing to something great," Marcus said.

Allen later said he had dreamed about the Heisman Trophy for years. But his dreams were not entirely grounded in reality. He told an interviewer he once thought an athlete could win the trophy in any sport.

"I'd play baseball and I'd say, 'I'm gonna win the Heisman.' The first time I knew it was for football was when O. J. won it." That was in 1968, when Marcus was eight years old.

He also mused about his fate. "Who could imagine?" he asked. "This kid from a not-so-well-to-do area of San Diego. I wanted to be rich and famous. But this, I just can't imagine. I've been on *The Today Show* and *Good Morning America*. I didn't know it was like this."

Following the announcement, Allen went back to Los Angeles, where he tried to relax. To share the biggest moment of his life, he arranged for his family to come to New York for the Heisman presentation. His parents had had to watch TV to find out that Marcus had won the trophy. The secretive Downtown Athletic Committee had not even permitted Marcus to phone home before the announcement was made. Now he would be able to make it up to them.

With so much excitement jammed into such a tight schedule, it wasn't surprising that there was one little moment that proved to Marcus that he was still mortal. It happened as he backed his car out of the driveway as he headed for the airport on the way to New York. As Marcus slipped the transmission into reverse and lightly touched the accelerator, there was a grinding sound. He had forgotten to close the car door, which struck some shrubbery and tore a hole in the door. For that oversight, as Marcus told Los Angeles *Herald* writer Jack Disney, he awarded himself the "Numbskull of the Month Award."

Quite unlike the award he was about to pick up in New York, the numbskull award was a gag originated by O. J. Simpson and some friends. Marcus had won the thing once before. He and O. J. were dressing for a black-tie dinner at Simpson's house. They put on their shirts, socks, and shoes first, so they wouldn't wrinkle their suits. Marcus was nearly done before he realized he had forgotten to bring his tuxedo with him. After a good laugh, Simpson found a substitute.

Marcus made sure to take his tuxedo with him to New York. This was an occasion when everything was to go right. There would be a gala dinner, attended by previous winners of the Heisman Trophy, and Marcus planned to proudly introduce his family to them.

When the big night came, coach John Robinson watched delightedly as Marcus executed his game plan. "It was a joy to behold," Robinson said. "Marcus always treated people well and made them feel relaxed. There's always a gleam in his eye and some humor in him. And on Heisman night, Marcus took the place by storm, escorting his family around the room. I guess little Darius [his kid brother] was the biggest star of the evening."

There were 13 relatives and friends, including Red and Gwen Allen; the other Allen children; and USC teammates Roy Foster, Don Mosebar, Bruce Matthews, and Todd Spencer. "We're awfully proud of Marcus," Red said. "But this isn't the biggest thing in our lives. You know what thrills me the most? I've got three sons attending different colleges at the same time. Now that's what makes a man proud."

Marcus Allen's grandparents had reason to feel proud, too. This was a family that played together and prayed together. Marcus once said that he thought it was ridiculous when he had to adhere to a 12-o'clock curfew in the 12th grade. But this was a tightly knit, supportive, and religious family. "My grandmother and my grandfather, they would make sure," Marcus once said. "A lot of times I wanted to stay home and watch football on TV [instead of going to church]. Their answer was, 'Go to church.'"

It made the entire Allen family proud to hear some of the tributes that were accorded Marcus. Leon Hart, a Notre Dame lineman who had won the Heisman in 1949, said, "Marcus is a fine back who has everything going for him. Size, ability, and brains." Howard (Hopalong) Cassady, the 1955 winner from Ohio State, said, "I'm proud to welcome Marcus into our club. He's got the stats, the courage, and a wonderful personality." And Johnny Rodgers, the 1972 recipient from Nebraska added, "I remember presenting Marcus a trophy at Lincoln High School just before he was leaving to go to USC. I wished him well. I guess that's kind of an understatement. He's gotten bigger, faster, stronger, and better."

Even comedian Bob Hope got on the bandwagon. "Marcus carried so many tacklers with him that they have him listed in the Yellow Pages under 'Public Transportation,'" Hope said.

The USC backfield coach, John Jackson, recalled an early-season conversation with Marcus, who was already talking in terms of 2,000 yards. "I told him, 'Let's get serious,' and we both started to laugh," Jackson said. "But Marcus sets very high goals for himself and does what is necessary to reach them. He has something special that allows him to reach his goals."

John Robinson dismissed any doubts about the validity of what Marcus accomplished in 1981. "You just can't quarrel with the record," the coach said. "His 200-yard games became commonplace. If he had a 150-yard game, it was considered a bad game. Imagine that!

"He has set a standard that is so high, it is just plain shocking. He played in a great environment, but there's no way you can look at Marcus and say, 'Yeah, but. . . .' There are no yeah, buts."

Allen's friend, O. J. Simpson, may have put his accomplishments in perspective better than anyone else. "There is no doubt that USC had a great line this year," Simpson said, "but over the years, a lot of great football players have had great lines. Marcus did what no other player has done.

"There is no doubt that Georgia's Herschel Walker is a great player. He could compete with anyone under similar circumstances. But the best performance of this year or any year has been the performance of Marcus Allen. At the end of the season, he was as fine a running back as I have seen at any level of football.

"It just goes to show that with the proper commitment and hard work, there is nothing one can't do."

Only the pros remained to be convinced that Marcus Allen was truly one of the premier football players in America.

In his senior year, USC tailback Marcus Allen set a collegiate record by averaging more than 200 yards rushing in five consecutive games.

Marcus flies into the end zone for a touchdown against the University of California in 1981.

Marcus Allen with USC coach John Robinson, who called Allen "the best tailback I've seen."

59

Marcus Allen, the proud winner of the 1981 Heisman Trophy, flashes a happy grin.

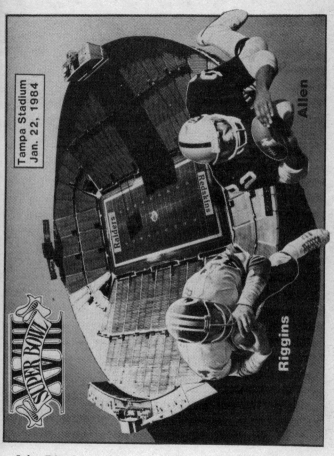

Tampa Stadium
Jan. 22, 1984

Allen

Redskins

Raiders

Riggins

*John Riggins and Marcus Allen carried their teams'
hopes into Super Bowl XVIII.*

When Marcus asked Al Davis to let him carry the ball more often, the Raiders' independent owner told him to run around the block.

The Raiders celebrate the first-period Super Bowl touchdown by Derrick Jensen, who blocked a punt and fell on it in the end zone.

The Raiders made life miserable for the Redskins'
John Riggins. Flattened here, he was held to 64
yards in Super Bowl XVIII.

In the third quarter, Marcus Allen (32) left Redskin defenders in his wake when he ran 74 yards for a record-breaking Super Bowl touchdown.

Wide receiver Cliff Branch leaps high to congratulate Allen after the longest run for a touchdown in Super Bowl history.

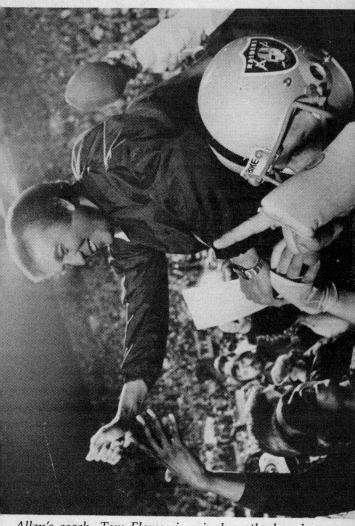

Allen's coach, Tom Flores, is raised on the broad shoulders of his players after the Raiders win the Super Bowl.

7

The Draft

The most eventful autumn in his life behind him, Marcus Allen went home to Los Angeles with the Heisman Trophy under his arm. Christmas was only a few weeks away, but there wasn't much more a fellow in his place could want — except maybe a win in a bowl game to wrap up his senior season.

The holiday calendar included another football game, the Fiesta Bowl, in which USC met Penn State. It wasn't a happy day for Marcus or the Trojans, who were defeated, 26–10. Allen gained "only" 85 yards on 30 carries, just the second time in his career as a starting tailback that he was held under 100 yards. He fumbled twice and several times was taunted by tacklers, who said things like, "Does that hurt? How does your head feel?"

Most superstars have to live with a certain amount of heckling and teasing from their opponents. Marcus has been around long enough to know that. But as he was about to discover, there were other slights that could be more bothersome.

As he traveled the banquet circuit in January and February of 1982, Marcus began to read articles quoting pro scouts who expressed some nagging doubts about his potential as a running back in the National Football League. In the months leading up to the late-April NFL draft, Marcus found his records and his reputation would not be worth a single yard in pro football. And worse, because of some questions about his speed, he had reason to wonder if his initial earning power would be reduced if he wasn't chosen among the top picks in the draft.

As the most honored college senior of 1981, Marcus was in demand all over the country. After the Fiesta Bowl came appearances in the Hula Bowl and the Olympia Gold Bowl. He was named the winner of the Walter Camp award and was *Football News* Player of the Year. Then in early February, he appeared in Philadelphia to pick up the Maxwell Award, second only to the Heisman.

Allen talked about the string of banquet dates he'd attended. "I'd be a great liar if I said I didn't enjoy it," he said. "But it gets pretty hectic. I've been on the road an awful lot. I think it's taking its toll. I'm kind of fatigued. I've got to leave here at six in the morning to fly to Dallas."

Marcus went to Dallas to take part in a pre-draft audition for several hundred NFL hopefuls. Present would be an army of pro football coaches, scouts, and trainers, all armed with stopwatches, scales, and measuring sticks of one sort or another. The pros wanted a close look at Marcus Allen and the other leading college seniors before they made their final decisions about whom to draft. Marcus was not in top physical condition for the testing in Dallas — what with all of the banquets and cross-country traveling. But he knew the pros would have enough data on him by draft day.

The annual draft of college talent has become a fixture of springtime, marking the beginning of a new year, just as the Super Bowl is the climax of every season. Because the draft is the league's lifeline, the source of its new blood, vast sums of money are spent in preparation. Each team arms itself with an encyclopedia of information on hundreds of promising and not-so-promising college seniors. The tool that is used to make sense of all this information is the computer.

Computers have been a part of life in the United States since the days of World War II. But until the 1970's, computers were used mainly by government agencies, banks, and insurance companies — institutions with multi-million-dollar budgets and files on millions of people and accounts. With advances in technology, computers became smaller, less expensive, and easier to adapt to the needs of smaller businesses. Among the first to capitalize — at least in pro sports — was the National Football League.

The Dallas Cowboys, the most visible team in the NFL, became widely known for their use of computers. The Cowboys were said to use computers for nearly everything, from analyzing game plans to processing the payroll. But no task was more important than stockpiling and sorting data for the NFL draft. Soon every NFL team was feeding into its computer every fact it could come up with on every potential pro player in college football.

To expedite the collection of material, various pro teams had invited college players to visit their headquarters. And that was why Marcus was going to Dallas one day in mid-February. Scouts had been studying and measuring him, and all the other players, for a couple of years. They were relentless in their hunger for more and better information to punch into their computers.

Sometimes it's easy to forget that computers don't make judgments. They perform calculations and process information at speeds that would take one person several centuries. But computers don't think. They don't draw conclusions. They are only as good as the information that people program into them. Computers can be wrong if the data they receive is faulty. In the weeks preceding the 1982 draft, the computers kept spitting out facts and figures that seemed to indicate that Marcus Allen was not the prime player in the draft.

Among the scouts there seemed to be a feeling that his lack of explosive acceleration, and the absence of a dominant offensive line such as he had at USC, would somewhat curtail his potential in the professional game. One scout put it like this: "Marcus Allen is a lot better than I thought he was before the season, but he worries me. There are some runners who have the instincts to elude tacklers, escape traps, and get you every inch possible. I don't put Marcus in that category."

Along those lines was the belief that he lacked the superstar potential of a back like O.J. Simpson or Tony Dorsett. Such runners had the ability to lead the league in rushing and to carry a team with their own brilliance. Almost no one seemed to suspect that Allen had such qualities.

Others debated about whether he would have an advantage in quickness over linemen and linebackers. One expert argued that the speed of the NFL's perimeter defenders would give Marcus trouble, because he was accustomed to USC's huge line blowing tacklers five yards down the field. Nonsense, said former USC tailback Mike Garrett. There's no way the NFL's 6-5, 280-pound interior linemen can be as quick as their 6-4, 220-pound counterparts in college football. Marcus could gain a step or two in the pros, Garrett said. "Because of Marcus' good lateral movement and good vision," Garrett noted, "he could be a classy back like Chuck Foreman [a star for several years with the Minnesota Vikings]."

What the pros seemed to like in particular about Allen was his pass-catching ability. That quality caused some scouts to rate him among the top two or three prospects, even though he was a bit lacking in size and speed. Allen wouldn't have to run the ball 35 times every afternoon, as he did at USC. A smart pro team would utilize him as a receiver, getting the ball to him in the open field, where he was most dangerous.

But still, the debate raged. Some scouts pointed to the disappointing performances by former USC Heisman winners Ricky Bell and Charles White once they became pros. Bell had one really productive year for the Tampa Bay Bucs before losing his starting job. White, who weighed only about 180 pounds at USC, got a little heavier in the pros, and the defensive linemen were able to nail him from behind.

On the positive side, there was the argument advanced by a Philadelphia Eagles' scout. "Marcus Allen's biggest asset is his ability to make people miss him in the open field, to create a void," the scout said. And a Dallas scout alluded to Allen's vision. "He knows when to cut and where to cut," the Cowboys' analyst said. "I saw him turn a five-yard loss against Oklahoma into a seven-yard gain. He couldn't have made that play in 1980 as a junior.

"I don't think he is going to be a consistent 1,000-yard gainer, but he'll get his 800 or 900 yards, and he'll be like Joe Washington of the Washington Redskins. He can run and catch.

Joe is a phenomenal receiver, but he is little. The fact that Marcus is tall, about 6-2, makes him an easier target to hit."

A Seattle scout made the point that while a lot of players seem to level off, Marcus was clearly improving. "And that's what you're looking for — a guy on a curve who's steadily getting better," the scout said.

USC coach John Robinson had some insights that the pros would have done well to heed. "I knew they were underestimating Marcus from the start," Robinson said. "A scout has to evaluate the tangible numbers, such as height, weight, speed, and so forth. Marcus was not the best in any of them. There was also the feeling that the environment — the mystique — made the USC tailback. But I saw him play so many big games and make so many big carries for whatever yardage was demanded."

Robinson, who was to become a successful coach with the Los Angeles Rams, had some further wisdom that the computer operators might consider in the future, when the numbers seem to suggest that a particular player is suspect. "Marcus does things with such ease," Robinson said. "He is calm and self-contained. But everything hasn't come easily. People see only the finished product. They don't consider the long, agonizing process of becoming a success.

"And the thing about Marcus was, his development was so gradual," said Robinson. "What impressed all along was his mind and his ability to understand the game. He's a very intuitive person. That gives him an edge, a leg up."

Now, try explaining that to a computer.

Bill Walsh, the coach of the San Francisco 49ers, said he thought Allen was the best back available in the draft. But most scouts tended to place him behind Baylor's Walter Abercrombie, Stanford's Darrin Nelson, and Arizona State's Gerald Riggs.

By the time the draft was held in New York on April 27, it was anybody's guess as to where Marcus would go. The draft has become such an important event that it is shown on television, and that is how Marcus and football fans around the country were able to follow the proceedings. The New England Patriots, with the first pick, selected defensive tackle Kenneth Sims of Texas. The third selection was Marcus Allen's teammate, USC linebacker Chip Banks, who went to Cleveland.

There were no running backs taken until the Minnesota Vikings used the Number 7 selection to choose Stanford's Nelson. Then the Atlanta Falcons, picking ninth, took Arizona State's Riggs. Next it was the turn of the Oakland Raiders. Marcus had a feeling.

The Raiders, after winning the Super Bowl in 1980, slumped to a 7–9 record in 1981. They ranked 25th out of 28 NFL teams in offensive yards per play. So they clearly needed a player who could enliven their attack.

Raider owner Al Davis had studied reel after reel of film. He came to the independent conclusion that Marcus Allen could run, catch, and block. He was quite pleased that Allen was still available when it came time for the Raiders to make their pick. And they didn't hesitate. Allen got the call, the 10th selection in the draft.

Raider coach Tom Flores provided some detail on how the Raiders, one of the most successful teams over the years in the NFL, viewed Allen. "His versatility hasn't been tapped yet because he's been primarily used as a runner," Flores said. "But he is also a good pass-receiver and blocker." To get Marcus, the Raiders passed by Baylor's Abercrombie, a bigger, faster back, who eventually was drafted by Pittsburgh. The Raiders gave Allen an edge over Abercrombie in versatility.

After learning where he would begin his pro career, Marcus said he thought he could be a starter right away. He added that he didn't expect to carry the ball as often as he had in college — no pro back can withstand the pounding of 40 hits per game that USC tailbacks must endure.

The Raiders considered Allen one of the three top players available, along with Kenneth Sims and Chip Banks. But they were careful not to create expectations he couldn't fulfill. "To say Marcus is going to be our savior wouldn't be fair," Flores said. "We're just not gonna put that kind of pressure on him or on ourselves."

Marcus made a favorable impression with his attitude. Of course, that had always been one of his best attributes. But it was never more apparent than when he described his approach to football. "I like to think every part of my game is weak, so I can work on it," he said. "The day you think you're okay is the day you'll have problems. I don't think any good back is ever totally satisfied, no matter how well he does or how well others think he does."

The Raiders awarded Marcus Number 32 and said they planned to use him in the same backfield with Kenny King, who wore Allen's USC number, 33. Flores compared the two of them to a backfield tandem from the days of the old American Football League. He likened them to Keith Lincoln and Paul Lowe of the San Diego Chargers. They were both players who could run inside and outside, and also catch passes.

By the time the draft and the postmortems were over, Marcus Allen had heard it all. "Some said I wasn't fast enough. What do you have to be? Does a pro back have to have 9.1 sprinter's speed? I heard I was too small, and then Gil Brandt said I was too tall. After a while people believed that, maybe, I couldn't even run.

"In some ways all the negative stuff served as inspiration. But actually, I didn't care after a while. I don't think many people can predict that an athlete is going to do this or that."

Maybe not. But a few months later, 49ers' coach Bill Walsh provided an enlightening postscript to the whole debate. "This makes me sound like a know-it-all," Walsh said, "but my opinion was that Marcus Allen was clearly the best player [back] in the draft. He has everything it takes . . . everything. He might become the Most Valuable Player in the NFL for the next four or five years."

Now Marcus prepared himself for his introduction to pro football. He knew the toughest test of his life was about to unfold. He would have to prove himself to a bunch of hardened, proven professionals — the Oakland Raiders. He could hardly wait to get there.

But first, he embarked on a program at UCLA designed to build endurance and make him a step faster. It was the same kind of dedication he had demonstrated as a collegian at USC, where his improvement from season to season was pronounced. All that remained now was to sign a contract, and he would be a pro in the official sense of the word.

8

Pride and Poise

An air of uncertainty hung over the Oakland Raiders in the spring and early summer of 1982. The Raiders liked to bill themselves as the winningest team in professional sports. Over the past two decades, their winning percentage was better than that of the dynasties that had ruled some other sports, such as the Boston Celtics in basketball and the Montreal Canadiens in hockey.

Now, however, the Raiders were in the process of fighting and winning a legal battle against the National Football League that would allow them to move to Los Angeles. Marcus Allen, who was the first Heisman Trophy winner ever drafted by the Raiders, inevitably found himself affected by the uncertainty of where the team would be playing.

He was not unhappy over the prospect of playing his pro football on the same field — the L.A. Coliseum — where he had played in college. Before that prospect became a reality, however, he had to go through the trials of negotiating a contract, surviving summer camp, and proving himself to his new teammates. And there probably wasn't a tougher bunch of guys anywhere in pro football.

The Raiders didn't know what to expect from L.A. fans. For nearly 20 years, the Raiders had been one of the most intimidating teams in the NFL. With their black and silver uniforms and their eagerness to play the game as violently as the rules would allow, they were feared by some teams and hated by some fans.

Their owner, Al Davis, was perhaps the most independent man in all of professional sports. He did things only one way — his way. He was not afraid to sign players who had been rejected by other teams. He welcomed veterans who were viewed as being finished, or as having a bad attitude, or both. He was not an easy man to know, but his name and image were among the most familiar in the NFL.

With his 1950's-style hairdo, his ever-present sunglasses, and his refusal to wear anything but black and white clothing, Davis was truly a maverick among owners. He was out of place in the stately, refined boardroom atmosphere sought by his peers. He seemed to go out of his way to be different. But Davis was so successful and shrewd that he won grudging respect — even from his detractors.

That is, until he got the notion to move the Raiders from Oakland to Los Angeles. The league had a rule that required an owner who wished to move his team to first get the approval of the other owners. Davis decided to move to L.A., regardless of what the other owners thought. The result was a lengthy and controversial court fight in which Davis eventually prevailed. His prize was the Los Angeles market, with its population of more than nine million and its total of more than four million TV households. The Raiders would have to share the market with the L.A. Rams, who played their games 30 miles to the south at Anaheim Stadium. But Davis was certain his fight to take the Raiders to L.A. would pay off in a TV bonanza that would guarantee him the ability to always buy the best talent.

And that was where Marcus Allen fit in. The Raiders had enjoyed 17 winning seasons in their 19-year history before plunging from a 1980 Super Bowl championship to a 7–9 record in 1981. The offense desperately needed new firepower to meet the standards of Davis, who believed a team had to put fear in the defense with the threat of big plays. The Raiders needed Allen's ability to break a long run along with his talent for catching passes coming out of the backfield. With such a threat in the backfield, the deep passing game would become more effective.

And there was another thing Marcus would bring to the Raiders — charisma. A headliner. Los Angeles is a town with an increasing appetite for celebrities. Marcus Allen's glittering career at USC was perfect for a new team trying to woo an audience in a market loaded with sports of every description.

All of this was in the background as Marcus began thinking about training camp, the thing football players least like about their occupation. There are two-a-day workouts, round after round of meetings, and few diversions. The older players tend to keep their distance from newcomers. It's customary for the rookies to enliven evening meals by singing their college fight song. And on the field, it's not uncommon for anxious players to exchange a punch or two while coaches look the other way.

Training camp is physically demanding, and it's also monotonous. A curfew is in effect almost every night. And even if there were no curfew, many of the players would be too tired to stay up until the wee hours. Besides, the competition for jobs is intense, and only a few players can afford to take their jobs for granted. Rookies, even first-round picks, can't afford to let their attention stray.

Marcus Allen had an idea of what was in store for him, but still, he felt strong and eager as camp approached. His workouts at UCLA had made him confident. He was leaving the contract talks in the hands of his agent, Ed Hookstratten, who also represented his pal, O.J. Simpson. While Hookstratten conferred with the Raiders, Marcus kept a low profile. He was staying at the home of a friend, having a little fun at night, and avoiding controversy.

The feeling was that he would miss little if any of his first training camp.

The Raiders traditionally conducted their summer training in the Northern California town of Santa Rosa. Because of the heat, the place was nicknamed El Rancho Tropicana. On July 22, 63 rookies and several veterans checked into camp to begin two-a-day workouts. The only rookie who was missing was Marcus Allen. Coach Tom Flores, who had no control over the contract talks, wanted to get Marcus in camp as soon as possible.

To have a real understanding of the team's system, Marcus would need to see each play diagramed on a blackboard. Then he would need to watch it on film, go out on the practice field, and rehearse it. "Marcus will be able to cram and study and learn the plays — but that isn't enough," Flores said. "There's just no way to catch up."

That's probably true of most rookies. In the case of Marcus Allen, there was no real problem. Two days after he was due in camp, the contract issue was resolved and Marcus agreed to a four-year, one-million-dollar deal. He wasted no time getting to camp. The deal was announced at 5 P.M. Marcus flew from Los Angeles to Oakland and completed the trip by car. He arrived at Santa Rosa shortly after 11 P.M.

"The Raiders are a fair organization and they treated me fairly," he said after his arrival. Then Allen set about proving that he was a fast learner who would be able to help the team as soon as he got his hands on the ball. As Al Davis put it, "We don't worry about signing people. We just want to see Marcus in the end zone."

Marcus made a favorable first impression on his new teammates. This was a team that more than lived up to its motto, "Pride and Poise." The Raiders were not the kind of guys you could easily fool. They could spot a phony, or a player who simply didn't have the right stuff to fit into their tradition.

Veteran guard Gene Upshaw, one of the team's landmarks for more than a decade, studied the newcomer from the first moment he walked into the dressing room. He liked what he saw. "He didn't try to set himself above anybody else because he won the Heisman Trophy," said the team's elder spokesman. "Once he opened up and embraced us, it was almost immediate. We all liked him. He didn't come out of USC with a big head. I guarantee you that eight or nine years from now, you'll watch him and still think he's a rookie."

Marcus didn't go out of his way to court the favors of guys like Upshaw, but it was to his advantage that they warmed to him so readily. Upshaw was the team's player representative and, with his heavily padded forearms and crunching blocks, he was one of the leading offensive linemen in pro football in the 1970's.

"It's easy to see that Marcus is going to be a great one," Upshaw said. "There's not a guy on this team who isn't excited about playing with a back of his caliber. I usually don't pay attention to the draft, but this year I watched. As it got closer to the time we would pick and he was still on the board, I thought, 'What's the matter with these other teams?' Then it was our turn, and I knew there was no way we'd pick anybody else."

Mickey Marvin, the Raiders' other starting guard, quickly spotted the sparkle in Marcus Allen's eyes, and that was all he needed. "He's articulate, he's a good guy, and he's a winner," said Marvin. For a bunch of guys with a reputation for dealing out physical punishment, the Raider blockers proved to be a soft touch for the new kid.

Coach Flores also liked Allen's work ethic and businesslike approach to his new job. "The way they practiced at USC is similar to the way we practice here," Flores said. "It's the same type of tempo. He does little things when he gets the ball in practice. Instead of running 10 yards past the line of scrimmage in a non-tackling drill, he will run 20 or 30 yards before he pulls up and comes back. He'll give it that little extra that it takes to push yourself."

One adjustment Marcus had to make immediately was the position in which he lined up in the backfield. In college he lined up 10 yards deep as the USC tailback. Now, however, he was much closer to the line of scrimmage, just 4½ yards behind the football. "You don't have a chance to see nearly as much," Marcus said. "At USC I could see everything, even stunts [trick moves by defensive linemen] developing sometimes. All I can see here is our linemen's big behinds. But I'm picking it up pretty fast."

One day, as he was getting familiar with the routine of training camp, a sportswriter from Allen's hometown of San Diego came to Santa Rosa. The writer wondered how Marcus felt about playing for a team that was the biggest rival of the San Diego Chargers. In answering, Marcus showed how well he had made the transition from Charger rooter to enemy Raider.

"I always respected and admired the Raiders," he said. "I thought of them as intimidators. They had pride and poise, and I liked that. They played rough and almost vicious. I can understand why that wouldn't make them so popular down in San Diego."

Marcus, as a high school defensive back in San Diego, was known for his exceptionally crisp and aggressive tackling. But the fans in his hometown would need some time to adjust to the idea of Marcus Allen as one of the Raiders, who were viewed as the football equivalent of 40 Darth Vaders. Raider history is filled with colorful and violent players, going back to Ben Davidson, a towering defensive tackle who once broke the nose of New York Jets' quarterback Joe Namath. Even more ominous was defensive back Jack Tatum, whose savage tackling was long a source of controversy, and was responsible for putting wide receiver Darryl Stingley out of football with a broken neck.

Of more recent vintage, there was defensive end Lyle Alzado, a fearsome 260-pound specimen who liked to scare quarterbacks by threatening to separate their heads from their shoulders. And he was just the start of the cast of outrageous and villainous characters who composed the Raiders' defense. Linebacker Ted Hendricks, who had been playing pro football since Marcus Allen was in elementary school, was nicknamed "The Mad Stork." He stood 6-7 and had frighteningly long arms that could snare ball-carriers and block kicks with equal effectiveness. He had a madcap approach to life that delighted his teammates. Once, to enliven practice, he put on a suit of armor and rode a horse onto the field. He had recently won an award as the player who best exemplified the spirit and pride of the Raiders.

There were some younger, but no less skilled intimidators on the Raiders' defense as well. Tackle Howie Long was just beginning to establish himself as one of the top pass-rushers in pro football. His aggressiveness seemed tailor-made for a team like the Raiders. Linebacker Matt Millen was the team's leading tackler and a source of worry for opposing backs. In the defensive backfield, there was Lester ("The Molester") Hayes, who made his reputation in part by covering his arms and jersey with a sticky substance to help him hold onto the ball. The NFL later outlawed the stickum, but Hayes remained one of the top pass-defenders in the league.

The Raiders' offense also featured some interesting personalities, as Marcus soon discovered. At quarterback was Jim Plunkett, a stocky veteran of 12 years who had known the jubilation of winning the Rose Bowl and the Super Bowl. In between, he had known the despair of quarterbacking losing teams, getting traded, losing his starting job, and being viewed as over the hill. But, as he had done with so many other players, Al Davis gave Plunkett a second chance. And in 1980 Plunkett quarterbacked the Raiders to a Super Bowl win over Philadelphia.

Plunkett's receiving corps featured Cliff Branch, a veteran wide receiver with sprinter's speed, and Todd Christensen, a rapidly improving tight end. Christensen was an intellectual who liked to quote Henry David Thoreau. Marcus Allen would also become a prime target for halfback passes. Helping to clear a path for him would be fullback Kenny King, who had played his college football at Oklahoma in the shadow of a Heisman Trophy winner named Billy Sims.

Put them all together, and the result was a football team that couldn't be bullied or threatened by any situation. They were a swashbuckling mix of individuals, lashed together in spirit by the genius of an outlaw owner. "Al Davis is a great owner," Marcus said. "He cares about his players. He takes in problem players and gives them a chance to play, and it has worked out. We're individuals, but we're not 45 dress-alikes. I like that because I'm an individual, too. But I know when we run out on the field, we're going to get booed sometimes. I can hear it now."

The Raiders were going to be facing an unusual situation, practicing in Oakland and playing their regular-season games in Los Angeles. Until their L.A. practice field was complete, they would be forced to commute 400 miles each way every week. But the hardship seemed to draw them together. More troubling was the prospect of playing before fans who seemed to have only a halfhearted interest in them. Los Angeles was going to take its time warming up to the Raiders.

Long before the Raiders felt comfortable in Los Angeles, Marcus Allen had been fully welcomed into the fold by the team. "He fits in real nice. He's like one of the family," said veteran offensive lineman Art Shell. "And when he gets that ball in his hands, he makes your eyes get all big and wide." The Raiders didn't know it, but they hadn't seen anything yet.

9

Rookie of the Year

That old feeling came over Marcus Allen again. That feeling familiar to all athletes, the feeling of nervous excitement that precedes every big game. It visited him the first time he ever stood in the tunnel of the Los Angeles Coliseum. He told a writer he was so nervous, waiting there as a USC freshman for the moment when he would run onto the field for his first game, that he almost turned around and went back to the dressing room. Now he was set for his first game as a pro on his old field. What player wouldn't have felt a few butterflies?

Training camp offers few pleasures. But one of them is the chance to play against someone other than teammates in exhibition games. The exhibition season, though meaningless in most respects, affords players the pleasure of performing before a live audience in a realistic environment.

Marcus Allen, after impressing his team-mates in the opening phase of camp, did well in the first two preseason games, although he played but one quarter in each of them. Allen rushed nine times for 52 yards and caught five passes for 44 yards. But a bigger moment lay just ahead as the Raiders got set for their debut in the Los Angeles Coliseum. The first two games had been on the road. Now the Raiders and Allen were going home — to what, they were not certain.

"I'm excited. It means a lot," Marcus said. "At the same time, I can't dwell on it. I'm returning to take care of some business. I'm not in college. I want to look ahead."

In that first game at the Coliseum, the Raiders scored a 24–3 win over the Green Bay Packers. Allen gained 41 yards on nine carries. Fittingly, he scored the first Raider touchdown in L.A. The fans seemed reserved, in contrast to the boisterous crowds that had watched the Raiders for years back in Oakland.

"The guys asked me what it would be like here," Marcus said. "It made me feel good, them coming to me. They called it Marcus' backyard. No, I didn't ask what the atmosphere was like back at the Oakland Coliseum."

There were 40,906 fans in Marcus' backyard, but there were also 13,362 fans who bought tickets and stayed home. Some of them had not received their tickets in the mail because of complications resulting from the sudden move.

While the Raider business office struggled to correct the ticket situation, the preseason was nearing an end, and the Raiders were about to begin one of the more unusual seasons a team had ever experienced. They were going to play their home games in L.A., but because they didn't have a practice facility in their new hometown, they would have to practice 400 miles away in Oakland. This meant that the players who didn't have homes in the area would have to live in a motel during the week. Then everyone would board a plane on Friday or Saturday and fly either to Los Angeles for a "home" game or to some other city for an "away" game. Marcus had bought a new home in Los Angeles, but he wasn't going to be spending much time in it for a while.

As if this situation didn't create a hardship, there was the lingering uncertainty over how the fans in L.A. would react once they got some prolonged, up-close exposure to the Raiders. And there was also the looming specter of a strike by the pro football players' union. The union wanted to upgrade salaries and working conditions in the wake of a new television contract that would add millions of dollars to the owners' income statements.

Against this backdrop, Marcus Allen made his professional debut. It could hardly have been more exciting if written by a Hollywood scriptwriter. In a 23–17 victory over the Super Bowl champion San Francisco 49ers, Marcus gained 116 yards (the most by a Raider back since 1977) and caught four passes for 64 yards.

Marcus made a couple of moves that delighted the Raiders. Once he made an abrupt U-turn, which he called just a spur-of-the-moment reaction. "It's not as easy to reverse like that in the pros," he said. "I've got to learn to disguise some things better and turn the sweeps faster."

Fullback Kenny King, who had played halfback until Allen took over, predicted more 100-yard days. "When he was at USC, I thought it was the offensive line," King said. "But I learned on the first day of camp that it was Marcus Allen. He takes off on a dime and wiggles past tackles. I'm not at all jealous of him. I'm just glad he's here."

Bill Walsh, the 49er coach who had been one of Allen's biggest boosters, quickly predicted Marcus would be Rookie of the Year. And owner Al Davis had a hard time restraining his enthusiasm. "I think he's a classic, great all-around back," Davis said. "But it's early. We still have a long way to go."

Another aspect of Allen's talent went on display when the Raiders traveled to Atlanta and blitzed the Falcons, 38–14, in the second game of the season. He completed a 47-yard pass to Cliff Branch that set up a touchdown. He also made a remarkable scoring play. The Falcons were in a blitz, which meant Marcus would have to block a linebacker. Then he circled out of the backfield into the flat, caught a short pass from quarterback Jim Plunkett, burst past two tacklers, and leaped over two more into the end zone.

After two Raider victories, Marcus had

gained 172 yards rushing, fourth best in the conference, and had caught eight passes for 103 yards. He was well on his way to making all the doubters eat their scouting reports. Only one thing could slow him down — a strike by the league's players. And that was what happened. On Tuesday, September 21, the NFL Players Association voted to strike. Ironically, it cost Marcus a trip home to San Diego, where the Raiders were scheduled to play the next Sunday.

When the strike began, the best guess was that it would last only a few weeks. Most teams remained in their home cities, and the players practiced on their own. But the strike proved to be far longer than most people had expected. The end of September passed without progress at the negotiating table. Some players got discouraged as October dragged by. Marcus remained in Oakland for seven weeks before deciding to return to Los Angeles and practice on his own.

"It gets difficult to work out these days," he said. "Each week a game is canceled and you ask yourself why you're still doing this, and sure enough, another game is canceled. You get discouraged." Marcus didn't stand to gain economically if the players won a wage scale — one of the key issues in the strike — but he seemed to be in support of the players' union. However, what he really wanted to do was play some more football.

The Raiders' new practice facility in L.A. was nearly ready in late October. But Coach

Flores said the team would probably continue to work out in Oakland after the strike, because there would be fewer distractions. The question was, When would the strike end?

At last, in mid-November, a settlement was reached, and the 57-day work stoppage was ended. The Raiders had four days to get ready for their first game on November 22, which would be against the Chargers at the L.A. Coliseum. It would be the first game in nearly two months and it would also be the first regular-season "home" game for the Raiders.

It was a strange game, by any definition. A crowd of 42,162 — about half of the Coliseum's capacity — showed up just in time to see the Chargers establish a 24–0 first-half lead. The crowd was not very excited after waiting so long to see the vaunted Raiders. But this happened to be a Monday night TV game, and the Raiders are next to unbeatable on Monday nights. With Allen producing two of their four second-half touchdowns, the Raiders rallied for a 28–24 win that extended their incredible Monday-night record to 18–2–1. Marcus, who gained 87 yards on 18 carries, scored twice in the third period on runs of three and six yards. He also caught five passes for 37 yards. Now THIS was what the fans had been waiting to see.

So far, with the exception of the strike, everything had gone almost perfectly for Allen and the Raiders. They were 3–0 and had every reason to be confident. Marcus came in for a little kidding from Raider end Bob Chandler.

"We made it clear to him when we got back from the strike that if he's in shape, he'll carry us and we'll go all the way. The pressure's on him. We just have to fill in the spots."

But a letdown seemed inevitable, and it arrived on the fourth Sunday of the strike-shortened season. The Raiders, after playing Monday night, lost some practice time to Thanksgiving and a travel day that took them to Cincinnati. They wound up losing to the powerful Bengals, 31–17. The Bengals concentrated on shutting down the L.A. rushing attack, and they succeeded. Allen was held to a total of *no* yardage on eight carries, by far the most ineffective game of his career, at any level. He did catch six passes for 54 yards, but turnovers and penalties combined to help beat the Raiders. For consolation, Marcus turned to O. J. Simpson, who recalled a game in which he was stopped with minus-10 yards. "At least I broke even," Marcus quipped.

The following weekend, Allen broke a couple of impressive runs against Seattle as the Raiders returned to form with a 28–23 victory. One of the runs was a 33-yarder on which he escaped from four tacklers. The other was a 53-yard sweep that set up the winning touchdown. For the afternoon, Allen made 156 yards, two touchdowns, and believers out of the Seahawks.

Mike McCormack, the Seattle coach, was stunned after seeing Allen on film. "He'd be going toward right tackle, and then all of a sudden he'd be breaking off left tackle, and you'd swear they cut some frames out of the film," McCormack said. "He's here and all of a sudden he's over there — boom."

Seattle players were talking the same way after seeing Marcus in the flesh. Defensive tackle Manu Tuiasosopo discovered how hard it was to pull down Allen with one arm. "I missed three or four tackles," he said. "You've got to hold him up and nail him. To slow a runner like that down, you've got to hit him and continue to hit him. That boy is remarkable."

The Raiders now had an impressive 4–1 record, and Allen had some impressive statistics. He had rushed for 415 yards, the third best in the American Conference; and he had scored seven touchdowns to lead the AFC. He was building momentum, just like the Raiders, who would face the Kansas City Chiefs in game Number 6.

A championship-quality team finds a way to win, even on a bad day. The Raiders were not at their best in Kansas City, but won, 21–16, on a 35-yard touchdown pass to rookie end Calvin Muhammad with 25 seconds left in the game. The Chiefs did a good job of containing Allen, holding him to 47 yards rushing and only one pass reception. In a season as long as the NFL's, there will be games like that.

Still, the praise for Marcus Allen continued to flow. Bob Chandler called him a carbon copy of Simpson. "I've never seen anybody so close to O. J.," the Raider receiver said. "I'm talking about everything — speech, mannerisms, the ease with which he deals with people, toughness, his whole approach to the game. The talent is his own, but it's uncanny the way he reminds me of O. J. When Marcus goes in for a touchdown, he even drops the ball the same way O. J. did — exactly."

One thing Marcus had that Simpson lacked in his early days in the NFL was a quality line and a solid defense. The Raiders looked like one of the top teams in the league. And they demonstrated it again by defeating their crosstown rivals, the Rams, 37–31, in a game billed as the Battle of Los Angeles. Allen was magnificent. He ran for 93 yards and three touchdowns, and caught eight passes for 61 yards. But it wasn't until the final minute that Marcus and the Raiders prevailed. Marcus ran two sweeps, one for 14 yards, the other for 11 yards and a TD, to win it for the Raiders with 29 seconds left. Allen felt a bit sluggish until late in the game, but when the contest was up for grabs, "he was unbelievable," according to Coach Flores. The heroics by Marcus helped the Raiders clinch a spot in the playoffs.

There was only one regular-season game remaining now. In it, Marcus ran for just 16 yards, but caught five passes for 91 yards and two touchdowns in a 27–10 win over the Denver Broncos. But before the playoffs were to begin, the Raiders had to take on the Chargers again in a makeup game necessitated by the strike. The Raiders posted a wild 41–34 victory over the Chargers in San Diego to finish with the best record (8–1) in the AFC. Allen gained

126 yards and scored two touchdowns, the second of which clinched the win for the Raiders.

Afterward, Coach Flores summed up his emotions by saying, "There is no question that God blessed us by giving us Marcus Allen." For his part, Marcus could only add, "What more could I ask? A Super Bowl, I guess."

It seemed like a reasonable request, but it wasn't to be. At least, not in his rookie season. The New York Jets saw to that, knocking the Raiders out of the Super Bowl chase with a 17–14 win in the second round of the playoffs.

The game, billed as the most important in Los Angeles in a decade, drew a near-sellout crowd of 90,037 to the Coliseum. After trailing 10–0 at halftime, the Raiders came back to seize a 14–10 lead, thanks in part to a four-yard touchdown run by Allen. But the Jets' defense did an excellent job against Marcus, holding him to 36 yards on the ground and 37 through the air. And a 45-yard touchdown pass from Richard Todd to Wesley Walker eventually won the game for New York.

It was a disheartening way for the season to end; but still, it had been a storybook year for Marcus Allen. One year after winning the Heisman Trophy, he was named pro football's offensive Rookie of the Year. He finished the season third in the AFC and fourth in the league with 697 yards on 160 rushes and scored a league-leading 11 touchdowns on the ground. He added 401 yards and three touchdowns as the Raiders' second-leading receiver.

He also was selected the only rookie starter in the Pro Bowl. No wonder some people were saying Marcus Allen was a guy who might redefine the position of running back.

In making his successful transition from college to pro football, Allen encountered few, if any, real problems. As he told sportswriter Jack Disney, "My background at USC placed me in pretty good stead here. To me, pro football is really not that complicated. Not when you've had such good training in the fundamentals. You'd be surprised how many guys lack them — there are linebackers who never covered guys coming out of the backfield. They get to the pros, and they don't even know how to backpedal."

Teammate Mike Davis said he had never seen anybody with the knack for making a cut and turning upfield so naturally. Marcus also proved to be courageous. He withstood some late hits without flinching. "Guys try to intimidate you," Marcus said. "It just makes me want to play harder. I can assure you, they don't scare me."

Marcus Allen had convinced everyone now. He was fast enough, he wasn't scared, he didn't need that mammoth USC line. All he needed now was a Super Bowl ring.

10

Calm Before the Storm

Marcus Allen had plenty of reason for optimism in the summer of 1983 as the Raiders prepared for their annual assault on the Super Bowl. Recent history had been kind to him. For three straight seasons, the graph of his progress curved sharply upward: 1980 — over 1,500 yards rushing in his first year as the USC tailback; 1981 — over 2,300 yards rushing and the Heisman Trophy; 1982 — the NFL's Rookie of the Year. And it seemed to Marcus that things would probably continue to improve. There was no immediate reason to think that his second season would be a trying one.

"We really are too diversified on offense for teams to key on me," he told an interviewer during training camp. "I honestly think I will have a better season than I did last year. Here's my thinking. First, I've got the year's experience under my belt. We played just about all the top teams around the league. I've got those first-time jitters out of the way.

"I was confident last year, but there were still some butterflies. Now I've got some experience, more knowledge of our offense, and more knowledge of other teams' defenses. I really feel more confident.

"One thing I want to improve is my blocking. I also want to be a better runner and pass-catcher and I believe I can. I can see myself having a very successful, productive year. You see, I think positively."

In the early weeks of the schedule, Marcus may have discovered a flaw in his reasoning. It became apparent that other teams *were* going to key on him. They *were* going to rig their defenses to limit his breakaway runs. The second time around would not be as pleasant. Marcus would need all the tools at his disposal to remain as one of pro football's most dangerous players.

The Raiders opened the season with a 20–10 victory over the Cincinnati Bengals, which they followed with a routine 20–6 decision over Houston. It wasn't until the third week that Allen had the kind of game people had been anticipating. In a Monday night game against Miami, Marcus and the Raiders defeated the Dolphins, 27–14. Marcus gained 105 yards rushing as the Raiders improved their Monday night record to 20–2–1. As defensive end Howie Long observed, "When it's dark outside, we're fantastic."

But more frustration lay ahead. The holes in

the line Allen had become accustomed to as a rookie weren't showing up with the same frequency. Everywhere he went, Marcus was shadowed by one or two defensive players. "They're looking for me now," he said. Despite a lessened contribution from Marcus, the Raiders were able to keep their offense working fairly well. They defeated Denver, 22–7, in the fourth game, and then barely lost to Super Bowl champ Washington, 37–35, in a game Marcus missed with a hip injury.

In his unaccustomed role as a spectator, Allen was one of the few non-Redskin fans in a standing-room-only crowd of 54,016 in Washington. The Redskins built a 20–7 lead before the Raiders surged back, scoring 28 points, including a 99-yard touchdown pass and a 97-yard punt return, to take a 35–20 lead midway through the fourth quarter.

Then Washington scored two touchdowns and a field goal in the final seven minutes to win the game. There was a lot of pushing and shoving, especially by the Raiders, but the Redskins weren't intimidated. They were impressed, however. "I wouldn't be surprised if we met them again in the Super Bowl," said Redskin guard Mark May. After this game, a lot of people felt the same way.

But the game had some negative consequences for both Marcus and the Raiders. On that 99-yard touchdown pass, wide receiver Cliff Branch pulled a hamstring muscle. He would miss more than a month, and the Raiders' big-play offense would suffer. Take away the home-run threat, and opposing defenses would be able to pay even more attention to Allen.

He commanded attention of a different sort as the Raiders bounced back from their loss to Washington with a 21–20 win over Kansas City. Allen grabbed the headlines he had grown accustomed to in recent years with a display of versatility few backs in the league could match. He rushed for 53 yards, caught six passes for 58 yards, and completed two passes, both perfect spirals, one of them for a 21-yard touchdown. Oh yes, he also recovered a fumble for the winning touchdown.

Allen set up the first L.A. touchdown with a 28-yard pass to fullback Frank Hawkins. In the third quarter, he delivered a 21-yard scoring pitch to Dokie Williams. "The guy covering Dokie turned his back," Marcus said. "I figured he would be open. It's amazing what you can do sometimes. Even though I got hit, I watched the ball all the way.

"I like throwing the ball. I just don't like getting hit afterward. I kind of appreciate what Jim Plunkett goes through every week."

In the fourth period, with the Raiders trailing, 20–14, Allen trailed Hawkins into the end zone and, when Hawkins fumbled, fell on the loose ball. "I hadn't been in the end zone in some time," Marcus said. "I had to get there one way or another."

If there was only a hint of frustration in those words, the feeling became more pronounced later in the week as the Raiders prepared for a game with Seattle. After six games Marcus had rushed for just 346 yards, compared to the league-leading total of 787 by rookie Eric Dickerson of the L.A. Rams, and 531 by another rookie, Curt Warner of Seattle.

"The yardage is tougher to come by," Marcus acknowledged in a talk with Seattle writers. He denied being jealous of Dickerson, who was getting to run with more frequency in a Ram offense put together by former USC coach John Robinson. "I think their offense is really built around him [Dickerson]," Allen said. "The Raiders don't actually change anything. They've been successful with what they've done and you fit into it."

Marcus was averaging just 15 rushes per game, less than half of what he was accustomed to in college; and he admitted he'd like to have the ball more often. He made his feeling known to Coach Flores, who replied that he was still learning how to best exploit all his talents. "Coach said he's still feeling me out," Allen said. "Sometimes I need 15 carries just to warm up. When you carry more, you get in the groove and feel you can't be stopped.

"They [the coaches] say they don't want me to get beat up. They want to keep me around."

The Raiders couldn't be faulted in that thinking. After all, they were the team that had the foresight to draft Allen when nine other clubs had passed on him. And Marcus still recalled the sting of being overlooked and underrated. "A lot of people underestimate me," he said. "I think I have a lot of desire, the intangibles, a lot of heart. At the risk of sounding overconfident, I was very confident. I really felt I could do the job. It really disturbed me that some people said I couldn't play."

Seattle was one of the teams that passed on him in the 1982 draft. A year later the Seahawks took Warner, who proved to be just what their offense needed, as Marcus had done for the Raiders. "He's got the magic," Marcus said admiringly a couple of days before the Seahawks handed the Raiders a 38–36 defeat. Allen gained 86 yards, his second-best effort of the year, but it wasn't enough to prevent Seattle from capturing the first of two wins over Los Angeles during the regular season.

The Raiders did not let the first loss to the Seahawks get them down. A week later, they took on "America's Team," the Dallas Cowboys, and won a thrilling 40–38 victory. Just as their earlier loss to Washington had been hailed as one of the most exciting games of the year, their triumph over Dallas received the same rave reviews.

"One of the greatest games in Raider history," Flores said. He went with a new starter at quarterback, Marc Wilson, and the strategy paid off with 318 yards and three touchdowns. Fullback Frank Hawkins provided 118 rushing yards, and Chris Bahr kicked a 26-yard field goal in the final minute to win it. For all the thrills, it was not a memorable game for Marcus Allen. The Cowboys limited him to 55 yards on 15 carries and forced two fumbles.

One of them set up a Cowboy field goal.

Allen's troubles continued the following week, when Seattle again whipped the Raiders, this time by a 34–21 score. Marcus gained only 30 yards and committed a costly fumble that led to a Seattle touchdown. "You're our leading scorer and the other team's leading scorer," said Raider linebacker Ted Hendricks, wielding the needle at practice a few days later.

After nine games of his sophomore season, Allen now had rushed 138 times for 517 yards, compared to 697 the year before. He had three 100-yard games as a rookie, but only one thus far in 1983. And his long gains were down. As a rookie he had runs of 22, 30, 41, and 53 yards. His longest in 1983 through nine games was 19 yards against Houston. In trying to explain the dropoff, analysts blamed the Raiders' offensive line, which was said to be inconsistent, and credited opposing defenses, which were continuing to give special attention to Allen.

Much to his credit, Marcus had caught 26 passes, despite seeing some double coverage, and had also thrown two touchdown passes. "Marcus is a great runner, and we're not going to stop giving him the ball or throwing him the ball," Flores said. "We're going to give it to him any way we can. Total production is the way I look at him. He's that kind of back."

Owner Al Davis sounded the same theme. "He's doing more things better than ever," Davis said. "He's a leader, and you can't measure that by statistics. He's one of the few good backs in the league who will block, and he's always been a threat to throw. He has been a great back all of his career."

Still, it wasn't until the Raiders had marched through the remainder of the regular season with a 12–4 record and reached the playoffs that Marcus was able to truly reassert his greatness. He wound up the season with 1,014 yards rushing and nine touchdowns, ranking seventh in the American Conference. He also caught 68 passes for 590 yards, good for seventh in the AFC. A 43-yard touchdown pass against San Diego gave him a total of three TD passes, quite rare for a running back. Marcus would have liked to average 25 rushes per game, as did Dickerson of the Rams, but he had to be content with 18 snaps per game. But he derived consolation from the arrival of the second season — the playoff season.

Things were overdue to start going Allen's way. And in a 38–10 romp over the Pittsburgh Steelers to open the Super Bowl drive, Marcus was the Marcus of old. He rushed for 121 yards and two touchdowns, including a beautiful 49-yard scoring play. The Raiders were just as impressive. In one of their finest performances since moving to L.A., they delighted a crowd of 90,334 with a nearly flawless show: no fumbles lost, no interceptions, just two penalties.

"It was amazing to look around and see all the seats filled," Marcus said. "That really motivates you." He appeared especially motivated on a four-yard scoring dive on the first play of the second quarter that put the Raiders ahead, 14–3. That score all but assured the

Raiders of a playoff meeting with Seattle, which would be their third clash of the season.

Although Al Davis was not thrilled about facing Seattle again, the Raiders hastily established there was nothing to worry about this time. The Raiders gave Seattle's Curt Warner a taste of what opposing defenses had dished out all year to Marcus Allen. Warner, the leading rusher in the AFC, was shut down with 26 yards on 11 carries after gaining 74 and 101 in the earlier wins.

Meanwhile, Allen attained a season-high of 154 yards rushing and 62 more on seven pass receptions. He was effective early on trap plays and later on runs outside. He got off a 43-yard dash that set up the final L.A. touchdown, a three-yard pass from Jim Plunkett to Marcus. The final score: Raiders 30, Seahawks 10. For his afternoon's work, Allen wound up with 216 total yards and a cut under his right eye, suffered on a blocking assignment.

Allen had proved himself before and now he was proving it again, under the most demanding conditions, the NFL playoffs. Marcus had helped engineer a berth in the ultimate game, the Super Bowl. On the biggest stage available, Marcus Allen would get the chance to prove to everyone who ever doubted his skills that he was the Number 1 all-around back in the NFL.

11

Superstar

There is probably more written and said about the Super Bowl than any single sports event in America. It commands the largest television audience. It probably attracts more gambling dollars. It certainly creates more pregame hype than any other contest. For two weeks leading up to the game, thousands of sportswriters, TV and radio crews converge on the site of the game and ask the same questions over and over. It can get pretty silly at times.

As Super Bowl XVIII in Tampa approached, many commentators took the approach that this was one game that didn't need all the hype. Although many Super Bowl games had turned out to be dull and lifeless, this one shaped up as perhaps the most intriguing ever. It would match the two teams that had clearly established themselves as the best in the National Football League in 1983. The Washington Redskins, the defending Super Bowl champions, were 16–2, while the Los Angeles Raiders, who won the league title in 1980, were 14–4. Based on the October meeting between the teams, a classic game was anticipated.

Each team had a style of its own. The Redskins, with perhaps the biggest offensive line anywhere, featured a resourceful quarterback, Joe Theismann, and a diesel-powered running back, John Riggins. The Raiders, on the other hand, were more of a quick-strike offense built around the multiple talents of Marcus Allen. There were any number of other facets to both teams that received in-depth attention before the game, but most experts reduced it finally to a clash between Riggins and Allen.

Riggins, a 240-pound veteran who was starring in pro football when Marcus was still in junior high, provided the Redskins with perhaps the best short-yardage runner in the game. During 1983 he rushed 375 times (third highest in NFL history), gained 1,347 yards, and scored a league-record 24 touchdowns. He accumulated 100 of Washington's 165 rushing first downs. In addition to durability, he provided dependability, too. He lost just three fumbles and was thrown for a loss just 12 times. Curiously, his rushing average, 3.6 yards, was rarely singled out for criticism, but it was .2 poorer than Allen's, and Marcus heard a lot of talk about the dropoff in his efficiency from 1982.

There was no question that Riggins had the more striking personality. Apart from Raider owner Al Davis, there were few individuals in the NFL with such a distinctive approach to football and life as Riggins. A year earlier at Super Bowl XVII, he turned up one day in military fatigues, then donned top hat, white tie, and tails the next day. And he then proceeded to run for a Super Bowl record 166 yards in Washington's victory over Miami.

In Tampa for Super Bowl XVIII, he showed up at a press conference wearing an Air National Guard jumpsuit. "You're probably wondering why I'm dressed like a clown, right?" Riggins said. "Well, last year the Redskins marched on Miami in the Super Bowl. This year we shall fly over L.A. The bombs will be hot and heavy in the first half, allowing our ground troops to position themselves to carry us to victory."

Someone asked Riggins what he planned to do about the Raiders' defensive end, Lyle Alzado, who was threatening to knock his head off. "That's a good question," Riggins said. "You know, when I went out on the field yesterday, I was looking for a soft spot, so when he knocks my block off it'll fall in a nice soft spot and won't get bruised up. And I hope he's enough of a gentleman to pick it up and hand it back. Besides, this head ain't been doing me much good the last 10 years."

The recurring theme of the pregame hype centered on how various players were going to maim, behead, and otherwise beat up the opposition. Alzado was the ringleader in this department, by a slim margin. Riggins, however, helped to put all this silliness in perspective by saying, "The Raiders have got this semi-reputation [for meanness]. Maybe they like it. But it's like their coach, Tom Flores, said. They go to church, they've got wives, stuff like that. They're not as big and ugly as people would have you think. They're a very hard-hitting team, but when the whistle blows, they stop."

Marcus Allen, who had been merely sensational in two Raider playoff wins, left the threats and the bluster to the other guys. He was quite content to wait for the game itself to make his presence known to a worldwide audience of hundreds of millions. And he wasn't being overlooked by football insiders. "He could be devastating," one analyst said. "He is right now running very hot, not fumbling, catching the ball very well. A dangerous guy in this game." Another scout added, "He is the most complete back in the NFL. He's an excellent receiver; he will block, throw the ball, and everybody knows he's a great runner."

Meanwhile, the excitement was building in Tampa, as free-spending fans from all over the country arrived to party and enjoy the festivities. One of the traditions of Super Bowl week is the official NFL party attended by 3,000 people. The theme this year was "A Night at the Circus." There were to be lions, tigers, bears, and trapeze acts, along with a menu featuring citrus-chocolate tarts and a dessert cocktail of ice cream, vodka, and Swiss chocolate-almond liqueur.

It was all part of an extravaganza that would ultimately be worth $175 million to the Tampa economy. That's the equivalent of about three national political conventions. We're talking big-time. One further note: Tickets to the game were priced at $60, but in some newspaper advertisements, people were asking $3,000 for four choice seats.

Even the Raiders got caught up in the pre-game hoopla. Seven Raiders were fined $1,000 apiece for arriving late at the club's first meeting of the week. The players claimed they didn't receive wakeup calls from the hotel operator. Said veteran linebacker Ted Hendricks, "It was just a matter of a couple of them being out and about last night and not coming in this morning. . . . Nothing bothers this team. This could happen to another team and they could totally collapse, but this isn't going to bother us at all."

After this one little incident, the Raiders settled down. They even started looking forward to practicing as a way of escaping the frenzy that had engulfed the Tampa Bay area. The Raiders had a particularly intense practice on the Wednesday before the game. There were several near fights and an offensive lineman got his nose bloodied. The Raiders were ready.

As game time approached, the serious analysis began. The Redskins had won the October meeting by two points, but Marcus Allen hadn't played that day. He was coming into the Super Bowl having gained 275 yards in two playoff games. If he didn't make the difference, then perhaps the Raider defensive secondary would. The Raiders were without two injured starters, cornerback Ted Watts and free safety Vann McElroy, when Washington rallied in the second half of the earlier game. Now Watts and McElroy were healthy again, and the Raiders had also acquired one of the top defensive backs in football, Mike Haynes, who came in a trade with the New England Patriots.

Washington's defensive backfield was viewed as a liability, with two inexperienced players, Ken Coffey and Anthony Washington, who had not started the first game but had won jobs since. The Raiders, who had lost speedy split end Cliff Branch to a pulled hamstring in the first game, had their deep threat back now. And they also had the league's leading receiver, Todd Christensen, who had made 92 catches during the regular season.

There were a couple of other nagging questions for Washington. Riggins was suffering from a slight case of the flu and missed practice the day before the game. And the Redskins' offensive line, nicknamed "The Hogs," had not been performing at peak form in the playoffs. Greg Townsend, one of the Raiders' defensive linemen, said The Hogs had looked "mediocre." Still, they were the most respected group of run-blockers in the league, led by 300-pound left tackle Joe Jacoby, 290-pound guard Russ Grimm, and 255-pound center Jeff Bostic.

The Raiders planned to make life hard for The Hogs by not lining up head to head, thus creating more difficult blocking angles. And they would try to force Riggins to the outside, where linebackers such as Rod Martin would be waiting. They would also rely on the strength of linemen Lyle Alzado and Howie Long to withstand the constant pounding of The Hogs and Riggins.

For all the reams of pregame publicity, no one was ready for what happened once game day arrived. A crowd of 72,812 jammed into Tampa Stadium, and a television audience in excess of 100 million saw the Raiders take command from the beginning. A blocked punt on Washington's first possession established the trend of the afternoon. Redskin punter Jeff Hayes, standing at his own 15, was unable to get his kick away in the face of a nine-man rush by L.A. Special teams' captain Derrick Jensen blocked the punt, which bounced toward the goal line. Giving chase were Raiders Lester Hayes, Kenny Hill, and Jensen, who fell on the ball in the end zone to put Los Angeles ahead, 7–0. Less than five minutes of the first quarter had elapsed.

Theismann, the Washington quarterback, had no luck throwing against the Raider defense in the first quarter, and things improved little in the second period. Riggins wasn't finding much room to run, either. And the Raiders didn't wait long to expand their lead.

Five minutes into the second quarter, Raider quarterback Jim Plunkett spotted flanker Cliff Branch speeding through the Washington secondary. Branch grabbed the pass from Plunkett and sprinted to the 15-yard line before he was overtaken. The two of them then teamed up on a 12-yard curl pattern to put Los Angeles ahead, 14–0.

What little offense Washington generated in the first half came on the following series, when the Redskins drove to the Raider seven before settling for a field goal that made it 14–3. Theismann, who would wind up the first half six for 18 for 78 yards, was victimized by the L.A. defense moments before halftime. With 12 seconds remaining, and the ball on his own 12, he tried to float a screen pass to halfback Joe Washington. But the Raiders, anticipating the play, had put a quick-footed linebacker, Jack Squirek, into the game. Squirek maneuvered to the outside, snatched Theismann's lob on the run, and scored to bury the Redskins, 21–3. The Redskins had used the same play and gained 67 yards in their first game against the Raiders in October.

Meanwhile, Marcus Allen, whose sore hip had made him invisible in that first meeting, was making himself known to the Redskins' defense. In the first half, he rushed 11 times for 51 yards. But it wasn't until the second half that he really shifted into high gear.

For a few minutes in the third quarter, it appeared Washington might be able to put together a comeback. They drove 70 yards in nine plays, with Riggins scoring from close range, to get to within 21–9 as the second half got underway. The Raiders answered with a 70-yard scoring drive of their own, aided by a pass interference penalty. Allen scored from five yards out to give the Raiders a 28–9 lead.

Although Washington had scored 17 straight fourth-quarter points in the October game, the Raiders weren't worried now as they grabbed control of the Super Bowl.

Perhaps Marcus had read what Redskins' defensive end Dexter Manley had said about him before the Super Bowl. "He's the kind of back that after we put some leather on him, he probably will pack up his shoes and take it to the house," Manley said. He could hardly have been more wrong.

On the last play of the third quarter, Marcus created a touchdown that would become the most talked-about of his life. All the skills he had been sharpening for the last four or five years came into play. His vision, his cutback ability, his extra speed. The play began at the Raiders' 26. Marcus took a handoff from Plunkett and started to his left. Waiting for him was Redskin safety Ken Coffey, who seemed about to dump Marcus behind the line of scrimmage.

"I thought we had a loss of yardage," Raider guard Mickey Marvin said later. "But when Marcus hit the hole, I said to myself, 'Look at that rocket go!'"

Washington's other safety, Mark Murphy, said he read the play too quickly. When Marcus suddenly cut back, Murphy had already advanced into the Los Angeles backfield. He, too, became a receding object in Marcus Allen's rearview mirror.

"The play is called 17 Bob Trail," Marcus said. "The tight end and tackle double-team the linebacker and the guard pulls. Mickey Marvin did a good job on his block, and I should have gone inside him. But I didn't and I reversed my field. They overpursued, and I guess they lost track of the ball. I found a hole and exploded through it."

Suddenly, he had burst out of the backfield, past the knot of linemen slugging it out in the pits, and was all by himself in the open field. As O.J. Simpson had said so many times, getting to that point is what separates the ordinary backs from the great ones. All Marcus had to do now was pretend he was back home, sprinting on the beach at Mission Bay, all the way to the end zone. "Darrell Green never saw me," Marcus said. "Once I realized that, I figured I could beat the rest of those guys."

When Chris Bahr converted the extra point, the score reached 35–9, and the issue was wrapped up. The Raiders added a field goal to make the final margin 38–9, the most one-sided game in Super Bowl history. Against all expectations, the Raiders had decimated the defending league champions. Riggins wound up with 64 yards on 26 carries, a 2.5 average. "The way the Redskins play football, they have to dominate the line of scrimmage, and they couldn't. When we're on our game, it can't be done," said Los Angeles linebacker Matt Millen.

And was Marcus Allen ever on his game! The one-year-old Super Bowl rushing record set by Riggins became the property of the Raider halfback. Allen had 191 yards to beat

Riggins' record, and his 74-yard TD was another record. To the surprise of no one, Marcus was named the game's Most Valuable Player. From Heisman Trophy winner to NFL Rookie of the Year to Super Bowl MVP in the span of three seasons. It was an unprecedented achievement, the supreme moment of Marcus Allen's career.

"I had thought about the MVP, but I really just wanted to win the game," Marcus said. "This is the icing on the cake. The Heisman Trophy was an award I'll cherish, but the Super Bowl is a team goal. I just happened to make some big plays. I don't think I've ever had a bigger game in a significant game like this.

"This is a different level. This is Number 1. This is an extravaganza. Records are made to be broken, but I'm going to enjoy these for a while."

Marcus had been somewhat overlooked, both by the Raiders during the season and by the media during Super Bowl week. When he had asked owner Al Davis to let him run more early in the year, he was told to run around the block. If he was hurt by that suggestion, he took it out on the opposition in the postseason.

"Mr. Davis said he was saving me for the playoffs," Marcus told a crowd of hundreds of reporters in the Raider locker room. "If I was overlooked this week, it didn't bother me. I just wanted to play. . . . I don't care what other people think, as long as Mr. Davis knows what I'm worth."

In the 10 seconds or so it took for Marcus to become a Super Bowl legend with his 74-yard run, he also became the personification of a lyrical description of his style he had made several years earlier.

"I do some things that trip me out sometimes," Marcus had told writer Alan Greenberg. "When I run, I am trying to do everything oh, so sweet. Running is like art. I like to throw a move on a cat like a paintbrush. Running is like painting. Let it flow. I want a Rembrandt to come out."

No one ever said it better.

About the Author

Chris Cobbs, a graduate of the University of North Carolina, is a sportswriter on the Los Angeles *Times*, for which he has covered, among other assignments, pro football, pro basketball, and baseball. In 1980 he wrote an article on drug use in the National Basketball Association that ran in many newspapers around the country, and he was a guest on the subject on the network television show *Good Morning America*. He previously worked on the Raleigh (N.C.) *Times*, the Atlanta (Ga.) *Constitution*, the Orlando (Fla.) *Sentinel*, and the Raleigh (N.C.) *News and Observer*.